UNDERSTANDING

THE

EVOLUTION

Of

YES!

Part 2
The YES! Trilogy

UNDERSTANDING

The

EVOLUTION

of

YES!

Insights for Affirmative Living

Allan C. Somersall Ph.D., M.D.
Author of "A Passion For Living"

Understanding The Evolution Of YES!

©1997, Allen C. Somersall, Ph.D, M.D.

Published By:
ProMotion Publishing
3368F Governor Drive
San Diego, CA 92122

(800) 231-1776

ISBN 1-57901-022-9

Printed in the United States of America

Books by Dr. Allan C. Somersall:

Your Evolution to YES!
- 111 Steps to Affirmative Living

Understanding The Evolution of YES!
- Insights for Affirmative Living

Evolutionary Tales from Dr. YES!
- A prescription of contemporary stories for Affirmative Living

A Passion For Living
- The Art of Real Success

Your Very Good Health
- 101 Healthy Lifestyle Choices

To
my mother,
who first taught
me to say

YES!

ACKNOWLEDGEMENTS

The author is indebted to several people for their valuable contributions that have made this book a reality: To John McIlroy and Dorothy Pilarski-McIlroy for many valuable discussions and significant work on the preliminary drafting; to my wife Virginia, for her encouragement and support through long, arduous nights as well as her valued criticism and editing; to Tara Guptill for most incisive insights and editing; to my agent, Carolina Loren, for arduous typesetting and computer editing, as well as for championing the work and guiding it through to completion; to Sophie Shena for typing and retyping the manuscript; to Patti Shaffer for useful comments. Without such a strong supporting cast, this book would still be an intangible dream. Thanks to each and all of you for your contributions. In the end, all remaining shortcomings are mine.

PREFACE

*The **YES!** Trilogy: The Evolution of **YES!***

This is your world, its length and breadth, its height and depth. It's all yours to explore. You have the right to be here and the privilege to do almost anything and to go almost anywhere. Yes, you do. So fasten your seatbelt.

Imagine yourself ... with your smiling face bathed in rays of sunshine and the thrust of rocket engines propelling you on your first solo flight into the unknown. This is the inevitable challenge for you to meet if you are ever going to take control of your life or to realize your dream. No more excuses, no more hesitation, no more dependence or delay. You must decide. You must commit, you must let go. The countdown is over and now you're taking off.

Up, up and away!

Imagine the freedom, imagine the fun, but also imagine the apprehension and fear ... That's all okay. You're soon soaring high, high above the surrounding crowd who seem content to congratulate you and to cheer your success.

As you soar upward, defying the downward forces of negativity and indecision, your adrenals are pumping furiously. Your heart is racing and your nerves and muscles are strained to peak performance.

You scan the wide horizon of opportunity with the eye of an eagle. You can see clearly now. You are in control, alone. This is it. This is living as you dreamed it could be. What a thrill!

You choose to celebrate the exciting moment with both thumbs up and a deep, clear affirmation that compels you to shout out loudly and deliberately... "y-y-YES!!!"

But you may not have always been this way. Perhaps you once drifted in the shadows of doubt, defeat and despondency. You were losing hope. Then you experienced an evolution ... *The Evolution of* **YES!**

Come trace this evolutionary journey as you go through this book and discover the secrets of such a transformation. Come and enjoy the scenery and the sensations along the way, but make it a personal adventure. Get involved with the prospect and the process of change. Real personal change. It will be an exhilarating experience of growth, fulfillment and joy.

The **YES!** *Trilogy* was written to be very personal and to strike deep at the core personality where we are all prone to be defensive and protective. It was designed for you. The form and content of each page of each volume was elaborated with you in mind. It contains a message distilled and delivered to your heart's address that you must receive.

You will get back to basics as you probe the space in which you generally live and might even sometimes hide. But there is nothing to fear in the inevitable exposé. You will be encouraged all along the way. You will sense that you belong and that you can become whatever you aspire to be. It's a recurring theme.

That theme deserves a further word of explanation.

EVOLUTION

The *concept* of evolution is a very useful one. It allows us to arrange an array of data and of ideas, first in order of sequence, in time or space, and then in order of complexity, in value or importance. It provides a mental picture for convenient examination and reference. It adds perception, pattern and process to ideas. It gives form if not substance, and it explains effect if not cause.

For these reasons and more, we will exploit its pragmatic value as a *concept* throughout The **YES!** *Trilogy*.

The Evolution of **YES!** is about a progression and in the case of any particular individual, it may even define a process. It is *not* about the origin of any species. It is about you ... your evolution. It is about your living today as an exclamation of all the positive, passionate and productive connotations implied by a strong, personal and affirmative **YES!**

It is about the origins of your personal style, the sources of your individual lifestyle and the way you choose to live your daily life. It is far more about practical psychology than about biology, with a spotlight on your attitudes and perspectives. It addresses your temperament and your degree of motivation.

These are critical variables. All such human characteristics are extremely important in determining the Life Equation: *What you put in equals what you get out.* It therefore addresses the real bottom line, yours included.

We will carefully trace a progression of responses to life that spans the extremes of **NO!** and **YES!** You will find a reflection of yourself somewhere along the continuum. That's guaranteed.

How do *you* now respond to life's challenges and opportunities?

- Are you prone to be negative? Do you tend to confess *"No, I can't"* before you even think?
- Do you feel left out, always looking on? When it's show time, is it always *"somebody else but me"*?
- Do you insist *"I should ..."* but somehow, it seems you just can't go beyond that conviction?
- Will you only act *"If ...?"* That is, will your results

depend on all the right conditions being met?

- Perhaps you *"would really like to"*, but that is only day dreaming. Do you have real passion and clear focus?
- Do you keep adding *"But ..."* and just making excuses, one after another, both good and bad?
- Do you have really good intentions for *"one of these days"*, but you're forever putting things off?
- Sometimes you can hardly make a clear or firm decision. Did you say *"Perhaps"?* Just maybe?
- You really want to, but are you *"shy"?* Always slow and apologetic in response and always evading the spotlight?
- You say "Yes", but are you content to just *"give it a try"?* Do you always have some reservation?
- Are you more committed than that, so that you will actually *"do your best"?* And is that ever enough?
- Will you respond with abandon? Will you affirm **YES!** and *"do it even if it kills you"?* There's a true **YES!**

Did you see a pattern? Did you recognize a progression? Could you even trace an *Evolution?*

However you characterize your response at this time, as you explore *The Evolution of* **YES!**, you will gain new insights that will inspire you to take affirmative action. The new perspectives should then give you a better understanding of how and why you react to life's challenges and opportunities in the way that you do now. Then with

v

practical suggestions and guidelines, you will be able to order your steps and keep moving. Eventually you will live out a superlative **YES!** Consistently so.

So follow each stage of development carefully.

YES!

Now, it is true that each of us would aspire and struggle to obtain a personal life characterized by positive thinking, buoyancy, passion, fulfillment and the like. Whatever your circumstances may be, you want to rise above them to experience, in principle, the best that is possible.

Health, wealth and the pursuit of happiness may not be truly your highest or strongest ideals. Presumably you also want a life of affirmation, not apology. There's a big difference. So you want to express not just a right to be here but the rhyme, rhythm and reason for being here. Well, the poetry, music and logic of life coalesce in a single, explosive word that says it all … **YES!**

Success is a three-letter word … **Y.E.S.!**

But what exactly does it mean?

This life of **YES!** will be described in detail as we progress through the evolving responses to life. And we cannot overstate the importance of the two *gigantic, little* words which form the bookends of this exploration: **NO!**

evolves to **YES!** as we traverse the grand dimensions of time, space and the human spirit.

All quality of life falls somewhere between these two polar extremes. It is a behavior pattern that we each adopt. Therefore, you can indeed characterize your own life even now by different stages or phases that dominate your responses to the challenges of today and every day. In this way, you define much of who you are and how you choose to live.

The Evolution of **YES!** will help you to put this all in context. You will come to appreciate that the quality of life you enjoy is largely yours to *choose.* It is a position that you take, it is a decision that you make. Your options can be as different as night and day.

On one extreme is the sad picture where one could experience life as a free fall in pessimism, negativism and defeat. This would be Phase One, a starting point. From this abyss, we will identify footholds or lifelines to hold on to. Then, from that dramatic beginning, we will trace an attitude to life that moves through progressive Phases towards affirmative and passionate living.

With vivid practical examples, we will consider common barriers to personal growth such as poor self-image, vicarious living, bad conscience, risk, wishful thinking, excuses, procrastination, indecision, shyness and more.

There will be a natural progression as each of these barriers is surmounted in turn. *The Evolution of* **YES!** will inspire you to rise above them all and to realize the best that you can possibly be. You will discover the life of **YES!**

The life of **YES!** represents the best that life has to offer. It defines a *positive mental attitude* that blends faith, optimism and assertiveness. More importantly, it defines a heart of *passion* that seeks to harness all the forces of imagination and the fire of human desire to become, to excel and to serve. It therefore also defines a life of *purpose and productivity*, a life that makes a difference and celebrates the joys of each moment as they connect into a pattern of growth and destiny.

TRILOGY

This trilogy of books began as a single volume, but the concept of **YES!** exploded in the author's mind as the gems of truth were mined. The continuum of change from **NO!** to **YES!** followed naturally along three orthogonal paths but retained a single pattern. It is a theme where fantasy, fact and fiction merge into a single three dimensional reality. That is essentially why *The* **YES!** *Trilogy* is synonymous with *The Evolution of* **YES!** It is three in one and yet one in three.

The heart of the message is clearly presented in Part 1, **Your Evolution to YES!**, where a compelling series of practical *Life Lines* is spelled out at each Phase. These *Life Lines* are all designed to help you get a grip on life and then keep moving along the course of evolution that consummates in Abandon. They are original, incisive and fascinating directives to follow. There you will discover the true life of **YES!** This is a perspective designed explicitly for the *pragmatic* mind. It is action oriented and you should aim to apply the *Life Lines* to advantage where appropriate.

In Part 2, **Understanding The Evolution of YES!**, there is a progressive series of insightful *Commentaries* to further elucidate, in each Phase, the issues and hurdles that one must overcome to get to **YES!** It explains in psychological terms why and how different responses to life's challenges and opportunities originate. But it goes beyond life's problems to identify solutions for affirmative living. This perspective is designed for the *probing* mind. You will want to construct your own analysis for sure. Try doing that.

In Part 3, **Evolutionary Tales from DR. YES!**, each Phase is illustrated by the portrait of a fictitious character in an original short story that will keep you guessing. This perspective is designed for the *pensive* mind. Each tale is more than just a tale. It is both a mirror and a makeover in poetry at the end. You should ponder the meaning and implications of each *Vignette* for your own life situation and response.

You will probably have a preference for one art form or the other. But the true or full content of this amazing metamorphosis will not be clearly seen until you grasp all three perspectives. So say **YES!** to all three parts.

You may begin reading the trilogy wherever you choose. A quick glance through the Table of Contents in each case will give you the guideposts which may identify for you a most convenient starting point. You could already know exactly where you have parked or met a roadblock in your response to life, and that would be a great place to get into the flow.

However, sooner or later you will want to cover the entire evolutionary path to **YES!** in the complete trilogy. Part 3 will pick you up on the earth, Part 2 will lead you to the horizon, and Part 1 will take you to the skies. From there you will shine like the star that you really are.

But you are admonished to take your time. Explore small areas at any one sitting so that you can discover all there is and apply the many practical suggestions. Read and re-read where necessary to internalize the precepts.

The **YES!** *Trilogy* is provocative yet practical, full of priceless quotes, interesting anecdotes and insightful social observations. The best principles of psychological theory are incorporated into a framework of self-reliance, with the motivation to live decisively and productively, while you remain controlled and relaxed.

After all, life proves to be truly exhilarating to those who, in any arena, learn to say a resounding **YES!** in the face of both challenge and opportunity. They are the ones who believe and commit to what they really want. They go for it with everything and they invariably find gold. So can you.

You must find the growing inspiration on every page, as picturesque illustrations will be woven into a beautiful mosaic of passion, truth and beauty. You will then emerge and finally affirm to live with conviction and enthusiasm, the exclamation of ..."**y-y-YES!!!**"

As you continue to grow and mature, you will get closer to becoming:

one hundred percent *positive,*
one hundred percent *passionate,* and
one hundred percent *productive!*

YES! You can. **YES!** You must. **YES!** You will.

YES! YES!! YES!!!

Contents

In the beginning...

NO!

1

Negativism

("No, I can't")

In the beginning ...

By definition, the process of evolution in psychological and emotional terms must begin at the downside, the dark side, the dull side of human existence. As much as I would love to avoid it, I cannot escape this dismal starting point. It is indeed a gloomy picture of negative people, in a negative world, thinking negative thoughts and engaging constantly in negative talk.

If you choose to avoid the negative altogether, you may want to skip over this introductory section and go directly to one of the later phases which follow. On the other hand, you may relate to your negative environment or wish to gain some further appreciation for the tenor of your immediate surroundings.

Yet many you reading this book will see aspects of your own lives through examples portrayed in this initial phase. You may need this exposé to help you get out from that crowd. The world already has too many other negative people.

NEGATIVE PEOPLE

The portrayal of any primordial state of mind or being can never be a good one. Ever since the real *Paradise Lost,* the human race has struggled and groped in darkness to regain emotional, psychological and spiritual health. We still remain outside of paradise, lost, lonely and afraid. That remains true of fallen man whether we consider the moral and spiritual dimensions or the physical, emotional and psychological conditions.

But for the purposes of this book, we are going to deal essentially only with the psychological-- the patterns of thought and behavior that define a quality of life which you and I choose by virtue of being human. We will consider the programmed script that projects onto the screen of our lives.

What *script?*

All students of psychology appreciate the experimental connection between thought and behavior. But they wrestle with the origins of the thought life. How do we come to self-image or imagination, to motivation or to values, and so on? Surely, we each have individual personality, from a very early age. As we mature, it seems as though our 'script' unfolds. But is it written in our brain neurons, or even in our DNA? Are we *by nature* what we really are - that is, on the inside, as it were?

Just imagine if you could get your hands on such a script. Would you not love to really understand why you are the way you are. Research is accelerating every day but we are still a very long way from home. However, there are some answers.

You do have a unique psychological script. You are a complex personality with multiple personas. You live with yourself most intimately. You talk and listen to yourself, on the inside. You are a drama unfolding, inside out.

As you are *nurtured*, the unraveling script takes on both new forms and new content. You are changed, constantly, often too, from the outside in. But that is not the good news. Rather, your script is subject most to the tyranny of your own will and determination. You are primarily the product of the choices that you make. You are a person in evolution ... Becoming.

So is your script essentially a decision-tree? Then how do you choose? By chemical algorithms in the brain? By emotional assertiveness or prejudice? By spiritual exercise?

Your script has been influenced from early infancy by both experience and environment. But the essence of personhood is your innate ability to edit it.

Theologians wrestle even more with *The bondage of the Will*. But there are some things of which all noble and virtuous pilgrims and seekers are sure. Life is more than DNA; it is spirit, it is mystery, it is destiny. That includes you.

How can we account for the diverse basic attitudes towards the challenges and opportunities that life offers? To answer, we are going to trace an *evolution* - the pattern of personal responses to life that actually span a continuum.

At the lowest end of this scale of life are **not** the poor and disenfranchised. but the truly negative people. They are the ones who evoke pity, not even compassion. They are without confidence or vision. Their life is out of focus. Their world is out of control. They are free-falling in an apparent abyss of doubt and pessimism associated with much apprehension and fear. Their attitude is so negative that all the joys of life are poisoned by some complaint or criticism and served in a cup of their own bitterness. Their hearts are cold. Their eyes are blind. Their world is barren. Their self-image is so poor that their own words echo off walls of frustration and paralyze their initiative.

"No, I can't," ... recycles like a mantra.

Remember, this is not the person at the bottom of the economic or social ladder necessarily. It is the individual lost and drifting in his or her own pessimistic paradigm that envelops self and surroundings in a dark cloud of denial, defeat and despair.

That is a chilling description which threatens to depress us before we even get started. But it is real. So many people experience life as a cold, lonely and hopeless existence with very few positive thoughts, little passion and no real productivity to boost their confidence or pride.

That is the bottom end.

Now, getting to **YES!** at the other extreme, which I am sure you would love to do quickly, is a process, a journey, an expedition if you like, demanding time and energy, as well as continuous personal growth. Many people never make it. They get stuck in the pitfalls of their early childhood experiences, or they trip on one of the land mines of the cultural milieu in which they now live. Or they simply give up. They could spend their entire lives buried in psychological caves of doom and gloom. Their joy and passion for living may have vanished at an early age, or some later stage of the life cycle, never to return. They may even share in the best of life's *toys* yet know little of its *joys*.

Hopefully, that description so far has little to do with the real you. It is all about someone else: your neighbor with the attitude problem, or the friend you know who dropped out of school, or the person at work who keeps messing up. But not you. You've never fallen that low. After all, you usually try to put your best foot forward and you're not doing too badly.

Really? Time out ...

Let's get acquainted early. How about you? Where do you fit in? What is *your* psychological make-up? What kind of world do you live in? Where do you call home?

Forget for a moment your physical address. Concentrate for a while on the impressions you have about yourself, your own personal sphere. It is your private mental space, yours alone. What is your psychological world view?

When you get up daily to greet the sunrise, what do you see? Is your world like a bottomless pit: a dark, foreboding place that is full of defeat, disappointment, depression and some other disaster waiting to happen? Are anxiety, boredom, criticism, doubt and escape, familiar companions that constantly whisper in your ear?

Or do you perceive the world to be full of diverse opportunity ... a place to learn something new, to connect with someone special, to express yourself with freedom and joy? Are you eager to be fruitful and multiply your passion for life, while you explore the wisdom of your mind within and the world of your milieu without, aiming to conquer them both?

Remember this: You do see things not as *they* are but as *you* are. The filter you look through is a reflection of the beliefs you have about the world you live in.

No two people have exactly the same set of beliefs, so no two people see the world in exactly the same way. Each of us has a private constellation of ideas and beliefs about the world that shapes our response to almost everything we engage in, from the mundane affairs of daily living to the major affairs of the heart that could and should bring passion and excitement to life.

Have you tried avoiding yourself by blaming everything on your negative world?

NEGATIVE WORLD

Before we examine some of the thought forms or beliefs that emotionally cripple so many unfortunate negative people, let's examine more closely how those beliefs are formed in the first place. What are the factors that shape the mindset or world view that you and I hold?

Our world view is formed out of the raw material of experience. Initially we form beliefs actively as a result of what we experience by way of personal contact and observation. We also do so passively through the information and influence of the mass media, and then vicariously through the thought and experiences of high profile personalities who, often unfortunately, shape public and therefore private opinion. In reality, you and I are human sponges, constantly absorbing new ideas and experiences, judging them to be good or bad and then forming beliefs that allow us to comprehend the world we live in.

It takes no sophisticated social analyst to arrive at the undeniable conclusion that a huge percentage of what we experience would be judged by us to be highly negative. Throughout our lives we are subjected to a constant torrent of negativity. We grew up with it. Hundreds of times each day we still suffer such shameful exposure. A lot of it was and is directed personally at each of us in one form or another.

This type of negativity is literally everywhere. We absorb large personal doses of this poison throughout our lives - from parents, teachers, coaches, clergy, friends, relatives and everyone else. Much of the "raw data" we take in comes passively from watching television and movies. Consider, for example, that by the time a child has reached the age of eighteen, he or she would have witnessed, on the screen, over twelve thousand murders, not to mention countless other acts of random and vicious violence. And what is dramatized on network television is reported for *real* on the nightly news.

Look anywhere, at anytime, and the prospect of seeing something awful and depressing is astonishingly good. This is the world we are born into, the world in which we make our home, the world in which we must struggle to find our place. That's our environment for you.

You and I also have our own set of direct experiences that help shape our worldview. We not only see and watch, but we also experience. And beginning as young children, those experiences are often overwhelming. So many children lack the nurturing they need to thrive as human beings.

Just think of the media's perception and projection of *The News*. It is a daily diet of all the negative events, portraying the worst of human experience for all to see and hear. Is that so because of the distorted sense of values in the public mind? Is it an attempt to make consumers feel better than the rest of the world, better than all the unfortunate victims of the worst inhumanities or simple misadventures? Why is there so much 'Bad News' on *The News?* Is that the lowest common denominator of humanity? There is always 'Good News' behind *The News.*

But we reap what we sow. Some observers want to stop the world; they want to get off. Suicide is the second leading cause of death in teenagers. That is the extreme response. These young souls cop-out, choosing to escape the pain and hopelessness they falsely perceive. Imagine the world view that a healthy sixteen year old must have in order to conclude that the world is such an inhospitable place that the only rational way to deal with it is by ending their own life. What beliefs would they have to hold, to be in that frame of mind? Did they feel useless, and think that the world was irredeemable and that no one cared? Did they imagine that their situation was completely hopeless and that the darkness would never lift? Did they find that life was a depressing, joyless, dead experience? Wouldn't they have to believe such erroneous things plus a few more? Sad! Shame!

That's the end point. That's where all this negative input leads. To powerless prey. It's a pitiful picture from a pessimistic perspective that can lead to a precarious plunge. That's the projected path into a pusher's program or a pimp's plans, all brought to you predictably but powerfully by the letter 'p', not on *Sesame Street* but on Main Street. That would be pathetic and unfortunately for many, it is also prophetic.

In the end, it still comes down to a battle of the mind. That's true for both young and old. As we think, we are. How do *you* think?

NEGATIVE THOUGHT

The late Rev. Dr. Norman Vincent Peale wrote an inspirational classic on "*The Power of Positive Thinking*". No one has dared to write its counterpart, for to do any justice to the power of *negative* thinking would be to describe such a dismal consequence as to make the swamp, the abyss of negativism that we are briefly alluding to here, look more like a paradise. It would be as if we reversed the polarity of every neuron in the brain to create chaos, confusion and complication not just in the head, but in the life of any such unfortunate individual. That power would destroy the essential nature of being human. It would kill all joy. It would distort all symmetry and destroy all beauty. It would tear relationships apart by distrust. It would stifle all imagination and inquiry, for fear of the unknown. It would suppress all human initiative and ingenuity and suspend all faith and hope. But I am falling into that same trap I so wanted to avoid.

From the earliest days of self-consciousness, children are inundated with facts and experiences that they are taught to perceive as being harmful or dangerous, simply bad for them. The combination of continuous exposure to the bad news of modern civilization and the negative judgments we form as a result of being exposed to them, set the ground work for the formation of a very negative set of beliefs.

If you think that the world is a dark, mean and dangerous place, it's no wonder ... That's what you've been taught. If you experience deep feelings of emotional insecurity, don't be surprised ... That's how you've been conditioned. If you think that it's impossible for you to have, to do, or to be anything more than what you are ... That's exactly what you'd expect. After all, how could you think otherwise, surrounded as you are by all the negative information and influences. And probably in your own experience since childhood, you've known some of the problems, the pain, and pathos of life.

This swamp is real. The constant negative exposure is real. The blanket negative condemnations are also real. Therefore, any self-defeating beliefs you have are ever so real. In struggling out of the swamp you would have to fight to rid yourself of some of your most ingrained beliefs.

The equation is a simple one. You are in large part the sum total of your beliefs, and if you believe that you can never do much, have much, go anywhere or be anything, that will be your reality.. Unless you act for change, you will live and die there, in the awful swamp of self effacement and world condemnation.

You must be careful not to condemn yourself all the time if you hold those beliefs. They are perfectly natural, yes, given the information and experiences you've probably been exposed to. But since you formed the beliefs yourself, you can decide to change them. Although the stimulus comes from your experience, the beliefs are still your own. You choose what to believe about yourself and your world.

People who are stuck, who just "can't" have, "can't" do or "can't" be what they want, are usually people who have poor **self-esteem**. In fact, poor self-esteem is one of the hidden thieves that can rob you of opportunity and action. People with low self-esteem already beat themselves up over far too many things as it is, without beating themselves up over having poor self-esteem too. After all, it is amazing that anyone at all has healthy self-esteem. When you think about the data the average North American has to deal with as they grow and mature, it is indeed surprising that any young adult can maintain a positive self-image or the mental attitude to cope. This deserves emphasis. We have observed that we absorb unbelievable amounts of negative imagery, negative information, and negative feedback. It is an avalanche. And it affects our self-esteem in incalculable ways.

But what do we mean by self-esteem? It is the integrated sum of both our self-confidence and our self-respect. It is an internal value judgment stating that we are competent in life and worthy of living. It is the foundation stone for personal growth and success. Let's just look a little deeper. This is not esoteric.

Self-confidence is indispensable to psychological health. We pride ourselves in our ability to do things and to do them well. Yet what we do is often less important than how well we do it. Self confidence is just as easily fostered through fly fishing as it is through heart surgery. We all want to be competent in the things that we do. Don't you? We all have a need to excel at something. If we manage to, that ultimately promotes a feeling of self-confidence.

Yet self-confidence goes much deeper than that. At its deepest level, true self-confidence is confidence in our ability to think rationally, to make the right choices for ourselves, to embrace the reality of any given situation and to deal with it effectively and efficiently. As Nathaniel Branden put it in *The Psychology of Self-Esteem*: "Man needs self-confidence, because to doubt the efficacy of his tool of survival is to be stopped, paralyzed, condemned to anxiety and helplessness--rendered unfit to live." That's true.

Self-respect on the other hand, complements our self-confidence. We all want to think well of ourselves. Don't you? We need to know that we have surpassed whatever mark we have set for ourselves when it comes to moral choice or personal standards. You and I have our own standards. When we live in a way that fails to reach those standards, our self-respect and therefore our self-esteem begins to fall.

With self-respect comes a sense of personal worthiness which is absolutely essential in developing self-esteem. When we think well of ourselves, when others think well of us and when we meet the standards we have set for ourselves, we plant seeds of life in fertile ground for our self-esteem to grow.

Speaking of fertility, just imagine what happened to your self-confidence and self-respect soon after birth. As you completed your journey down the birth canal and entered this world with a clean slate of consciousness, you had the opportunity to become grounded with feelings of both self-confidence and self-respect. After all, you made it. This should have paved the way for the self-esteem that you need to grow and develop. Or should it? You had to contend with contracting walls and much turbulence just to get here. You may have had to be manipulated, pushed and pulled, with the absence of all autonomy. Then almost immediately upon arrival, something horrible started to happen. You met face to face with the crushing realities of your new life. They smacked your little bottom just to set the tone for your submission and early capitulation. You arrived tiny, immature and dependent. You could not do anything right. You had little to offer or contribute to the world. You were fragile and vulnerable. So you cried. You made a mess. You cried some more. You got blamed by an impatient mother and a preoccupied father. When they got beyond their elastic limit they even spanked you. You rolled over. They said 'no' to almost everything you tried to do. You learned to say 'no' too. You acted out your frustrations. They wrestled with you. Then you stumbled and fell. You tried to explore your environment in ways you should not. You struggled in vain to express yourself. You tried to assert your identity and your will and at that point, they really did start to crush you. They limited your space. They ordered your time. You resisted. They called you names. You acted up. You hurt inside. So you fought back. You asserted '**NO!**'. That was probably your first word. Hopefully, it was not your last.

We contend with these and other antagonistic realities all our lives. Unfortunately, some people never quite grow up and they never win the battle. They are losers in the game of life. In the face of opportunity, they reiterate the same negative refrain: '*No! I can't*'.

Such negative self talk is always prophetic.

NEGATIVE TALK

If you are still in the habit of saying 'No, I can't', you might want to pause and reflect on what you actually mean when you say those words. Here are some possibilities.

No! I Can't SEE It. The Biblical adage says 'where there is no vision, the people perish.' Remember the old metaphor ... 'If life is a parade, one percent of us are in the parade, ten percent are watching the parade and the rest don't even realize that there is a parade.' Well, those trapped in the dark cave of "No, I Can't" are the ones who don't know there is a parade, who don't realize that life has possibilities or goals worth striving for. They don't see the beauty and the bounty in the world. They see only confusion and scarcity. They see survival as the only possible path to walk. They need to open their eyes; let the sunshine of hope, truth, beauty, love and opportunity illuminate their world to dispel the gloom and foreboding of such pessimism.

The sun is always rising, if you are awake. Are you awake? The sun is always shining, if you look for it. Are you looking? The sunlight is always shining to make everything manifest for all to see. Can you see?

Some claim to see but they cannot understand.

No! I Can't UNDERSTAND It. This self-defeating belief is rampant in people who have a formal education that is less than advanced. They see possibilities out there but they think the challenge is too complicated. They believe that special knowledge is needed to unlock the keys to success.

Knowledge which they of course don't have. Their self-image is so low that they have to look up to everyone. They hold to the belief that each successful person understood instinctively what was required to be successful. The idea of 'learning as you go' is a foreign concept to them. They want complete knowledge of the entire path before they are willing to take the first step. They hold to the belief that everyone else knows more than they do, and therefore everyone else is on the fast track, everyone else understands.

In fact, formal education has obvious limitations and lack of it is not a condemnation to a life of futility or even mediocrity. Is life itself complex? Is truth complex? Is opportunity complex? Just look around and assess your own heroes. Observe that it is always the simple ideas that pave the way to personal development and growth. The big decisions of life are not addressed in formal schooling. You do not need a Ph.D. to resolve the major issues of marriage, parenting, job placement, entrepreneurship, purchasing a home or making a good investment. And certainly, neither the choice of friends nor the nurturing of quality relationships require any formal training. In really important matters of life, the degree certificates on the wall are not the passports to effective or passionate living, much less to success. Just look around. You too have what it takes.

Some understand but they fail to believe.

No! I Can't **BELIEVE** *It.* The old adage that 'seeing is believing' was corrected long ago. We now understand that in areas of creativity, of performance, of personal growth and achievement, 'believing *is* seeing'.

Sure there is a reality ... a cold, obvious, physical, ever present reality ... for which seeing compels believing and for which *only* seeing will justify believing. It draws a line of truth which demarcates a boundary that only fools and those who hallucinate cross over.

But there is another reality, not immediately apparent yet no less present, for which believing guarantees seeing and for which *only* believing facilitates seeing.

If we only believed what we saw, all growth would cease. There would be no basis for analysis and insight, no reason for research or innovation and no hope for change and improvement. Unbelief would stop us dead in our tracks, for to move forward would be to encounter the unknown future, like an explorer entering a dark cave in the wild jungle.

Napoleon Hill has immortalized the words, "Whatsoever the mind of man can conceive and believe, he can achieve." History tells us so. Science and technology tell us so. Biographies from each generation have told us so.

'To believe' is to unlock vistas of opportunity that make life a daring adventure. It is to find hope in the possibilities of the future. It is to bring the perspective and power of the spiritual realm into the common marketplace where mortals strive for excellence and aspire for greatness.

Someone wrote that 'prayer is the key to heaven, but faith (belief) unlocks the door'. That is true in every arena of life. Doors of opportunity are all about you, if you would only open your eyes to see. And those very doors will fly open if and when you choose to believe: to believe in yourself, to believe in possibilities, to believe in the future.

Pascal said that 'human knowledge must be understood to be believed', but experience tells us that in all matters of real importance, truth must be believed to be understood. Even in the mundane routines of ordinary life, to believe is to liberate the mind, the personality, the life of the believer so that they can soar to heights of daring adventure and achievement.

Are you a believer? Do you believe that 'for every drop of rain, a flower grows'? What do you experience every time you 'hear a newborn baby cry, or touch a leaf, or search the sky'? Are you still imprisoned by unbelief that prompts you to confess 'No, I can't' in the face of the unknown? Choose to believe and live.

Some will even believe, but they may fail to personalize the very realities they perceive.

*No! I Can't **PERSONALIZE** It.* Think of how your dreams so often fade. It is as if you wake up to find that the best prospects of life were only an illusion. They evaporate like dew with the rising sun.

Sometimes you see the possibilities of the future. You understand what is needed and you even believe in the possibility for change and growth. You think that making a decision would be so easy. Through the compelling influence of family, friends or just convenience, You decide to make a personal resolution to pursue a new course of action.

When you make the decision, you seem full of enthusiasm and vigor. But after a while, it all starts to fade away. The original conviction vanishes. You give up. Then you are told that you lack perseverance. Perhaps you agree. But the result often reflects how you made the decision in the first place.

If you think about it, making a decision is a two part process. First, you make the decision. Second, you make it *yours*. If you make a decision without making that decision yours, you have not made a decision at all. It would be better to call it an 'agreement with a proposition' rather than a true decision making.

If you can't make the decision, the plan or the project your own, then you haven't really engaged yourself, or tapped into the inner resources you have. Instead, since you are totally at the mercy of external influences, when those influences wane, so does your decision. You haven't personalized it. You haven't made it yours. You haven't completely and totally identified with what you are trying to accomplish. So the reality is that "you can't" because "you can't personalize it."

Once you do integrate your plans into the very fiber of your being, once you have committed heart and soul to the completion of your project, then "No, I can't" will begin to disappear. In fact, the very act of personalizing a decision tends to be like a trigger to the imagination and to creativity. Waves of possibility seem to flood the soul. You become empowered. You feel a surge of inner strength like you can now move any mountains that remain in your path. You want to tackle the challenges at hand. And as you do, the mountains of doubt and opposition begin to fade away.

That will be true, if and only if you act ... if you do it.

No! I Can't DO It. But so many never get started on their exciting adventure into the unknown. They see the possibilities and understand what would be involved. They believe in the opportunity and even when they try to personalize it, they still keep telling themselves that they can't seize their moment. They can't deliver. Why? Because they have never done so before. They are untrained novices. They don't know *how*. That's the wrong emphasis.

After all, riding a bicycle is a habit. Typing on a keyboard is a habit. Writing by hand is a habit. You don't question your ability to ride a bike, type on a keyboard, or write a note to your grandmother. You know you can do them because you have done them in the past. But at one time you could do none of these things. *Doing is habit forming.* If you have a long history of success in accomplishing things in the past, you don't usually doubt your ability to complete things in the future. Do you? You have every reason to believe that the success of the past will be the success of the future.

But what if you don't have a long track record of success? What if you haven't had much success at all? Do you use that experience to create a belief that you can't do new things, or do them well, or even finish them? Sad to say, but some people often do. Then you should ask yourself whether that is a belief that makes sense. If it does not, then you should want to change it.

Let's pose the real question. And let's make it direct and personal, for you might be right at such a point just now. Here it is: 'If it is true that in the past you have not been successful, is it really true that this means, in the future, *you* can't be successful?' Answer that for yourself. The question is rhetorical. 'Of course not.' But did you find yourself unconsciously agreeing or saying 'yes' to that question? If so, you should ask: 'Why do I believe it? Is it a universal self-evident truth?' Of course not. It is a lie.

Think about it. Your future is indeterminate.

Your past record does not hold the key to your future. But your present response will unlock the door to your destiny. If you now let go of self-defeating beliefs about your ability to 'do anything' you will just start doing it. And the more you 'do it', the better you will become, and the more likely it will be that you will succeed at it. Furthermore, each success will breed more success.

Do I see you nodding in agreement? You can see your brighter future. You can understand the opportunity.

You can believe in the possibility. You can even personalize it and now you know that you can do it.

YES! YOU CAN!

Practice the art and power of affirmation. Think it constantly, say it loudly and live it daily. You will begin to move, to progress, to grow, and the reality of **YES!** will come into view.

But you must *participate*. Read on.

* * *

The Evolution of **YES!** *unfolds:*

You **Can!**

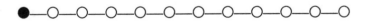

2

Participation

("Anybody else but me")

Slowly and almost imperceptibly, over the last half century, we have allowed ourselves to become a society of spectators. It is trite but true that time marches on, life goes on and the world looks on, with or without television.

In the initial phase of *The Evolution of* **YES!**, we commented on the negative role that television plays in portraying so much of the dark side of our world. That helps to create a pessimistic world view which when internalized, contributes to the roots of negativism typified by *"No, I can't"*.

In this second phase we want to consider a slightly different but related influence of television.

We become fans of what we see on TV. It almost becomes an addiction, for we become passive and obsessed with the action on the screen. We worship its heroes. We watch the box until we no longer know it's on. And then we watch some more. We watch everything: sports, games, movies, politics, news, weather, geographics, science, medicine, religion, crime, sitcoms, soap operas, commercials, cartoons and everything else.

In the early nineties, we even had the chance to watch a real war on television. Imagine, the live horrors of war reduced to just one more set of flickering images on a television screen for the world to see. Millions could tune in, sit back and "enjoy", with almost passive indifference to the human suffering, the sheer suspense and excitement of high-tech action drama, just as one would receive another Hollywood creation.

Just the posture of *watching* television has its own implications. Your eyes are riveted to the screen, unlike say, listening to the radio, where you can engage in simultaneous activity and still get it all. There is an implicit control with TV. You sit and absorb the action with callous numbness, unable to filter the myriad of contiguous images, real or imaginary, subtle or blatant. You internalize the messages by induction or osmosis, with little control or cerebral response.

Television is the consummate spectator activity.

It takes little thought or imagination to receive the television message. As Marshall McLuhan taught, 'The medium is (itself) the message.' We are victims of the involuntary electronic manipulation by the producers. Much of the time we contribute nothing but passive observation. There is no demand for any input whatsoever.

Consider an obvious example: The news camera operator takes the TV spectator by their eyeballs and directs their perspective on any real event. It is as if he or she says 'stand here, look at this; then move to the next scene or vantage point, but only at my discretion.' You therefore see the world through those lenses exclusively. Add in the editorial splicing, and the manipulation gets even worse. No wonder the media moguls exert such influence on the culture. They control the processing and flow of information and even the interpretive values in any modern society.

How unfortunate. In principle at least, you deserve your unique perspectives on reality. You should enjoy the privilege of not only observing the events that matter in your immediate world, but also the right to interpret them. More importantly yet, you should, and indeed can shape the course of those events by active involvement and participation. Yes, you are intrinsically designed for stardom in your own space and time. But you must not just admire. You must act.

Perhaps the innovation of interactive TV may provoke some kind of original action or participation in the future, but the nature of even that exercise may limit the input to the extent of mere video games.

Speaking of video games, just imagine the implications of consuming the formative years of school children in such a passive, mechanical fantasy. No creativity, no innovation, no imagination is being cultivated during such routine, repetitive hand-eye co-ordination movements. There is challenge yes, entertainment yes, interaction yes, but it predominantly favors the brain-dead. The mindless hours spent by this young generation will be paid for by the inertia of maintaining the status quo of many an enterprise in years to come.

To take this a little further, if video games were not enough, the technology of virtual reality threatens to exaggerate this spectator phenomenon even more. Now we can, by electronic illusion, observe even the unreal worlds of computer generated images. We thereby blur the margins of reality and fantasy, and almost lose personal identity in the process. We are absorbed into the medium but carried there as both spectator and passenger. What next?

However, there is some hope in these advances of technology. Perhaps the best glimmer comes from the exponential growth of the Internet. Now anyone can access large banks of information and become an active player in the process. You can surf and then you can dive in. Your presence can make a difference. In fact, a real difference. The interaction can be remote but no less real and that reality can effect change, real change. One idea can spawn an explosion. And who knows where that idea may originate? It could even be yours. So all is not lost.

But we must get back to the bare essentials.

Television and video games are not the only culprits.

Consider our ball parks, stadiums, theaters, concert halls and other amusement centers. Millions make regular trips to these modern temples to observe the gods of entertainment in all their glory and splendor. They cater to our appetite for vicarious experiences, while we present our offerings and make social penance in this multibillion-dollar pseudo-religious exercise. Stars and superstars are rewarded for their service with sinful adulation and ridiculous wealth.

You and I must also contend with the torrents of information (and misinformation) poured out daily in newspapers and magazines, popular superficial fiction, biographies, self-help books like this one, and other hypnotic fabrications of the printed page. We consume it all.

Now, if our purpose was social commentary, we could look long and hard at the effects of all this passive 'spectating' on community and family life. Chances are, the news would not be good.

But let's forget the community for a moment and think instead about you. How does all this third-party 'watching' and prolonged, passive 'spectating' affect your life?

There is an obvious yet subtle danger as far as I can see. You could run the risk of living an almost entirely vicarious life; of living an empty life in the shadow of other people who are taking risks and doing things, people who are responding to the demands of a full and active life. What a great tragedy it must be for anyone to reach old age and to have to think back on a life that was spent watching other people enjoy their thrills. Indeed, what quality of life can anyone enjoy if they live their life *watching* instead of *doing*?

FANS, FANS AND MORE FANS

The modern Olympic movement is an excellent catalyst to international cooperation and understanding between peoples, but it is far more than that. Every four years the best amateur athletes assemble, after years of arduous preparation, to compete fiercely (and we trust, fairly) for the highest athletic crowns. The world rises to cheer and honor true heroes who relish in just the right to participate, and then we almost kneel in awe at those who rise above the crowd to dominate their sporting events.

But the best stories usually come from off the track or field. Those are stories of courage and determination, of discipline and sacrifice, of faith and hope. Athletics is life on display. Yes, the athletes *live* while the world *looks on* from idle chairs of lethargy. They experience reality while we engage in fantasy. They enjoy adrenaline and sweat while we endure eyestrain and obesity.

Every four years World Cup Soccer reaches a climax and the pride of well over a hundred nations rises to a mad consummation. Millions if not billions, rediscover their roots as cities and communities on every continent erupt in rival celebration of each final goal. Then comes the insane reveling and ardent nationalism as each victory is celebrated and new superheroes are born.

But we can revel then only in the pride of collective consciousness since we make no individual contribution. The folks at home are just like outsiders looking in, not quite invited to the "real" party.

Each year, the fall classic World Series of Baseball, the NBA playoffs, the NHL Stanley Cup and the NFL Superbowl, all create wonderful emotional experiences for millions of fans who indulge their appetites for sports entertainment. But more so, the competitions provide repeated doses of an irregular visual narcotic or opiate (depending) for real people who suspend their own identity to enter into the projected lives and the unreal world of the professional athletes. We know them, but they don't know us. We love them, but they hardly know that any one of us exists. We are their *fans*, mere faceless consumers.

This is modern culture.

Who would imagine the popularity of televised golf? Yes, one might have imagined that even the professional PGA tour, or the many celebrity classics, should make poor candidates for popular TV. But the ratings prove otherwise. Come on down ... Tiger Woods! There are millions of people out there in armchairs, whose only experience of driving a golf ball straight down the fairway is the thrill of watching someone else do it. On TV.

In a different arena, just estimate the concert audiences when world class musicians and vocalists take to the stage after years of practice and rehearsal. There is adulation and wild excitement. Many more only sit back at home and listen to radio, compact discs and audio cassettes.

Or consider the many avid readers of National Geographic Magazine for example, whose only inclination to visit Asian temples, or to explore the Great Barrier Reef off the coast of Australia or the vast barren islands of drifting Arctic snow, is in staring at the spectrum of full color photographs that immortalizes that famous publication. They travel in home.

Shakespeare wrote,

All the world's a stage and every man's a player.
We have our entrances and our exits...

But in contemporary society, we should observe that the vast majority of people today only enter and exit the galleries of life's theater. Their only thrill in live theater is in watching someone else perform their role.

There is no question about it. Certainly, there are people in the marketplace giving life everything they have; people who are squeezing every last drop of excitement and adventure from the brief years they will spend on this planet. There are examples all over the world, but certainly not enough of them. There is a popular cliché that divides the entire world into three groups: those who make things happen, those who watch things happen, and those who seem to awaken and ask ... 'what happened?'. Their numbers differ by orders of magnitude.

The focus of this book and the complete trilogy is on getting to **YES!** We want to identify, to understand and to overcome the pitfalls that so many fall into, often unconsciously. We aim to explore hurdles or barriers which get in the way of embracing life with all that we have.

In the first phase of *The Evolution of* **YES!** we saw very graphically a mountain of negative images, data, communication and interaction that you must overcome, or at least tunnel through, before you can get into full gear on the journey to **YES!**

In this second phase, we have begun to move a step further to examine another trap to which many people fall victim. They combine passivity with self-pity and start to believe that a fulfilling life is only possible for *"Anybody Else But Me"*. The intent here is to help to get the couch potatoes off the couch and the fans out of the stands.

If you have remained on the sidelines cheering the parade, you *can* enter into the mainstream of life. You can go from the excuse of passive observation ... and into the excitement of live action. It is more than obvious that the real joy of life is in the *doing* not in the *watching*. Therefore, no matter what the size of the arena or whether the cameras take note, you must participate. You must find expressions of self to enter into real life.

How many times have you had the supreme thrill of throwing back your head, extending your arms, and saying, 'I did it! I really did it! I really and truly did it!'? You finally did the thing you elected to do, for the love of it. Those must have been blessed times.

Among the wealth of blessings that technology has bestowed upon us, one of the less obvious ones is that it has brought a plethora of fascinating and otherwise famous people and events right into our living rooms and into the town square. Naturally, our first inclination is to watch them. Then as we watch, we enjoy and we want to watch some more. The colors are bright, the action intense, the tension dramatic. So of course, we pull up a chair. We can't wait to see what will happen next. And commercial technology is forever busy creating more visual splendor, more special effects and more intense action.

But is television bad? Is it unworthy of our time? Is it unwholesome for our families and communities? Is this another old diatribe on the banality of that medium? No ... this has nothing to do with the TV screen per se. Television can be great entertainment as long as you don't fall into the trap that so many people seem to have succumbed to ... using television as a substitute for living. A way to pass time.

Watching to learn and grow is no great crisis. But some of us go further. We watch TV not just to learn, or to be entertained, or even inspired. We watch the box to enter into life through the lives of others. We want a piece of their excitement, we want a share of their passion. We enjoy their mastery, we identify to some degree if not completely, with their struggles. We feel privileged to enter into their extremes of agony and ecstasy. That is the vicarious life.

Your life ceases to be your own when it is lived entirely through the experiences of others. If you thus fail, you consign yourself to a hollowness that is sometimes difficult to detect. You become more and more idle. You live your life only in your mind, robbed of the opportunity to sing the song yourself, to swing the bat yourself, to express yourself by what you do. You have removed yourself from the joy and excitement of an active life, just by being a fan.

Fans can be very diverse. They actually represent a spectrum. Some fans engage in fantasy as observers but then they translate events into their own world. They learn the lessons of real life and go on to be *fantastic* individuals as they apply them personally and locally. Other fans get smothered by their own fantasies and go on to become real *fanatics.* They become at best, psychological perverts, incapable of expressing their own potential. Or at worst, they should be labeled as psychiatric patients, with marked affective or personality disorders.

Obviously, then, becoming a fan of some popular media personality in the field of sports, entertainment, politics or whatever, that is not the essential problem. It is the effect that you and I allow this experience to have. Let me illustrate with two extreme cases.

THE BEST AND THE WORST OF FANS

First, let me briefly relate the true story of one exemplary Canadian.

Peter Maker had a revival experience. He was a pretty good middle distance runner in high school. He enjoyed his track and field and excelled at it. But like a lot of people, once he was in the real world and life was putting him in a *full court press*, he reacted to the stress by drinking, overeating and smoking. Five years out of school, Peter was in excess of 265 pounds, smoking and drinking far too much. His lifestyle became totally sedentary.

On an average Saturday afternoon he would turn on Wide World of Sports and experience like a "real man", the subliminal extremes of "the thrill of victory and the anguish of defeat." All this he did while polishing off big bags of potato chips, flushed down by a six pack of cold imported beer.

One day, in the half alert stupor of prolonged television viewing, Peter was struck by an interesting race that he was watching. It turned out to be a marathon. At first he was going to flip the channel—'no need to be reminded of his old days at the track'. Before he did, something caught his attention. He was struck by his own admiration for the effort and dedication the runners had invested in preparation for this one race. He began to remember what it was like not just to *watch,* but to be out there pounding the pavement, putting in the miles and giving it everything you've got.

But it wasn't the winner that really captured his imagination. He was too far out of shape to identify with the winner. It was the runners who came later, spent in exhaustion, buckled over in oxygen-deprived agony, but holding on to the bitter end. They had made a choice just like he had made a choice. They had chosen to immerse themselves in their passion and to revel in participation. They had decided to commit to a punishing journey of hardship and pain that ends in personal fulfillment and pride. They had chosen the hard way, but nevertheless this was real life, real living. They were true heroes.

Peter could even imagine what was going through their minds as they crossed the finish line. 'I've done it! I've finished! I've given it my all!' And what was *he* able to say at the end of that same race? 'I've watched it! I've finished another bag of potato chips!'

Something began to stir deep within him. Peter could see that life on the couch would never get better. He was himself going from bad to worse. He realized that his was becoming an empty life, offering so much less than what it was really meant to be. Peter decided then and there that it was time to turn off the television, get out his sweat pants and return to the road.

He did. He was back running again.

It went slowly at the beginning but Peter didn't care. He had no agenda. He just wanted to get back to doing the thing he loved. He disciplined himself on a new workout program. He took responsibility and control, and entered back into life. It paid off.

Over time Peter started to excel. He trained, he strained to the limits of his potential, and in two years he was celebrated as the new Canadian Marathon Champion.

What an inspiration for the couch potato! *Fan-tastic.*

Now contrast that with the mournful plight of another, not so exemplary, Canadian. We all know of sad cases I am sure, but this one in particular comes to mind for me.

In 1976 as part of a sales reward trip, I took a vacation tour package to Las Vegas with my wife. On the connector bus from the airport, we had the irony or misfortune to sit beside a not so young woman who turned out to be most fascinating.

She was a true-blue Elvis Presley fan, who was flying to Las Vegas to watch her true love perform. In the course of conversation we discovered that she had spent every single vacation since age fourteen following Elvis around. Wherever he happened to be, she would get there, buy concert tickets for every single night and spend her entire vacation just watching him perform. She had a collection of every record Elvis ever made. She had seen all his movies many times over. She had accumulated his paraphernalia in all shapes, sizes and descriptions. Rooms in her home were decorated with posters, banners, pictures, articles ... all constant reminders of her teenage idol.

Although now married, she let it be known that there would always be room in her heart and her bed for the King. I can't imagine what her husband must have thought.

After we had checked into our hotel, my wife and I started making plans to tour the Calvada Desert the next day. We would rent a car and spend a leisurely day in the countryside.

After all, Las Vegas is like a ghost town during daylight hours but bursts into life--or an apology for that synonym--after dark. The nights in "Sin City" are filled only with gambling, entertainment and food. The .99¢ early morning breakfast is really a hypnotic snack before most patrons drag themselves to retire to bed—often broke and bored. That lifestyle must be meant for owls or bats, I thought.

But we were here nevertheless, so we at least could enjoy the environs if not the glittery interferons. We looked forward to our outing with paradoxical excitement. We invited our new acquaintance along.

Big, big mistake.

We left town in the middle of the morning and cruised up to the border of Nevada where it meets the state of California.

Strangely enough, the white compact Japanese car we had was scarcely adequate to contain the effervescence and animated conversation of these three tourists. But the chatter had nothing to do with the geography or history, as rich as that could have been in the Wild West. It was all interesting subject matter for psychology and sociology as our new friend shared her heart and soul.

She was thrilled to be in Vegas this weekend, after one full year of eager anticipation. She was going to see her heart-throb again tonight. She could hardly wait. After driving just a couple of hours, we arrived at the desert resort we had planned to visit.

No sooner had we had a quick bite to eat than our new friend insisted that she had to drive back to Las Vegas early, in the mid-afternoon. Time was of the essence. This had become an emergency--a psychological (or psychiatric?) emergency. She had to be the first one in line at every single concert she attended.

We decided it was pointless to resist even though we had the keys and the map. She had the passion and the need. Sad for us but shameful for her, I thought. Before we left, my wife made a promise to herself---to this day she has not told me what it was.

The next morning at breakfast it became apparent to us that our "friend" was in a trance, so we asked her what had happened. She told us about the previous evening's ritual. In the course of one of his songs, Elvis had actually looked her in the eye while she sat down front, a mere three or four rows back. The expression of rapture on her face as she relayed this fact to us was incredible. She tried to reproduce the moment by getting a good seat for all the remaining nights.

We later learned as we boarded the bus to return, that on the final night she spent the evening hours on her balcony, bathing her face in tears, while staring with tender love at the Hilton Hotel next door. That was where Elvis was staying. I considered that truly pathological, perhaps a personality disorder in her case.

That story is sad, but true. And if you knew the woman, it would be even sadder. She had a lot going for her: energy, commitment, passion. But she had chosen to invest it vicariously in a fantasy relationship with someone who didn't even know she existed. I often wonder what she did when Elvis died. Unlike Peter before, she was a *fan-atic*!

The truth is, she had a choice and so do you.

WHY NOT YOU?

So many people think that excitement, passion, and recognition belong only to the performers they observe. They fail to see that they can never get the same satisfaction from watching Martina Hingis charge the net at Wimbledon, as they can from stroking a clean backhand down the line on their own neighborhood tennis court.

As impressive as each return of the space shuttle may be, you would be more qualified to shout "Mission accomplished!" by learning to fly a small Cessna turbo prop at the local flying club, or even by building a small remote-controlled flying toy that traverses a mere 100 yards. At least you would get to control the stick. Anything that you can do is infinitely better than anything you can just watch. It is passion expressed. And that's life.

Are you given to being a spectator? Are you living much of your present life vicariously in the experience of your favorite sports team, movie star or TV personality? What fraction of your day and your life have you taken control of, in which to express your own passion and to follow your own dream?

Joy is in the doing; fulfillment is in the experiencing. Your best thrills are in taking personal risks. All these are not reserved only for the Academy Award winners, the Superbowl Champions or the Olympic medallists. They can happen for you anytime, even today, when you stop *watching* and start doing; when you turn off the technology and, as Goethe put it: "Plunge boldly into the thick of life". Why not trade in your TV channel converter and climb up on to your stage set?

You are invited to *come on down*, out of life's audience and into the live action. Leave the stands and get down on to the field. Participate. Why not make yourself the star? Why not bask in the glory of pursuing your personal passion with total intensity? Choose your own activity. Select your own arena. Determine your own awards. You can be yourself. You can do your thing. You can begin to achieve whatever you truly desire. Anytime. Anywhere. Anyhow. So begin your act today. Begin to stake a claim on the good life, the life that is waiting for you, the life that you were meant to live.

You do have the right to play. Just by virtue of being human. You have the right to be involved. You have the right to your own moment in the sun. You have the right to trade in your program even now, pick up your gear and get into the action. The experience of doing it yourself is not the prerogative of some few or any chosen people. We all have the right. You have the right to indulge life. Exhilaration and adventure are not designed only for all the people you watch. So climb off your chair ... you've got rights too. Leave behind the couch and jump in somewhere ... anywhere. By engaging yourself you are giving yourself the opportunity to have your moment of triumph, your own adrenaline rush of victory, your own experience: real, alive and all yours. Trade in *"Anybody Else But Me"* for "Anybody, Including Me!"

Yes, *you do have the resources to play*. You really do. Those resources might seem rusty. You might have to give yourself and your self-esteem a bit of breathing room to securely find them. But you do have a unique role in this world. You have a singular set of skills. You have a personal wealth of dormant capabilities that are irreproducible. You have latent talents piled high, one above the other, if you would only take a chance and put them into use. Get rid of your fear today.

For many people, a perceived lack of any talents or gifts is a real hurdle that they need to overcome. They tell themselves that the reason they spend their life *watching* other people is because 'those people can do things ... and I can't.' That's ridiculous. No one is born with star dust on their shoulder. At one time, even Pete Sampras, the No. 1 rated player in the world, did not know how to play tennis. Lunar astronauts once trembled at the prospect of their first short solo flight across an open field. Neurosurgeons once butchered cadaver tissues in early anatomy labs. They each had to learn; and practice; and improved; and persevere. At one time, Stephen King wondered if he would ever sell a single book. A similar comment could be made of filmmaker Stephen Spielberg or actress Meryl Streep, or legendary Oprah.

All of the stars you know had to make a start.

Recall Oprah's early days on TV. Her shows were quite shallow and almost meaningless in content. But Oprah grew. Her values and insights began to transcend the empty potpourri of social and cultural vomitus that her directors staged and which the audiences seemed to revel in and regurgitate. With time, Oprah went through her own evolution. Her own sense of responsibility to the public and her own commitment to excellence and to quality of communication, led her to rise above the base and callous milieu of her art form to become a shining light, a true role model for a generation of television viewers. She took risks. She took a position and followed it. And she emerged on top. She practised the disciplines of life before the watching world and insisted on taking the high road at every turn. She even learned that easy answers and short cuts would not effect real and lasting change. But she persevered. She assumed responsibility, took control and by clear dedication and hard work, achieved what so many others only dream of, or else watch others indulge in. She is a pace-setter, an icon in ebony and a testament to individuality.

In the same way, you also have to make a start. But don't expect to start at the top. And don't think that you lack what it will take to do your own act. You don't.

You also have a reason to play; a reason to get involved; a reason to engage. This reason has to do with everything that you are, the 'whatever' that lies buried deep inside, suppressed by pessimism from within and by criticism from without.

Another reason is that you're needed. You can make a difference. You can impact the lives of people around you. You can leave your own deep footprints on the sands of time, if only you would get walking.

But there is an even better reason to enter the mainstream of life, to let your passion flow. It's fun. It makes life full of zest. It causes you to spring out of bed every morning. It is the spice of life. It is the experience of a life that's truly worth living.

Certainly, you have a right to participate. You have all the resources that you need and some compelling reasons to play. You must aim to play the game of life hard enough to win. Whatever the outcome, you must agree that you *should* ... and that's the voice of **conscience**. That's next.

*   *   *

The Evolution of **YES!** *unfolds:*

You can
participate!

3

Conscience

("I should")

Human beings have an innate capacity that is apparently unknown throughout the rest of creation. We exhibit self-consciousness. It is as if we each live as a *compound* personality, not to be confused with a *split* personality. We are able not only to think and reason, but also to observe and judge ourselves. All the time we are either excusing or accusing ourselves for our thoughts, words and deeds.

You are most aware of who you really are by design, by intent and by performance. By design, because conscience dictates that you *should*. By intent, because you alone know what you *really* want. And by performance, because you observe *all* your own actions. It is possible to deceive others since your consciousness and your conscience are generally invisible. But you cannot fool yourself.

So the course of life is never unseen or unmarked

in its present reality. You know yourself truly, even if not fully. And that knowledge is demanding.   It demands accountability. You know you *are* and therefore you know you *should*. But your sense of *"should"* transcends your private world. It resonates with the awe and wonder in the external world which causes fascination and intrigue. It is personal but meaningful. Isn't it?

FASCINATED BY "SHOULD"

It fascinates me to observe that when I look up and see the sky above, complete with the moon and the stars, I observe the one true bond of all humanity. It is the one perspective we all share, a common vantage, a common enigma. And we all have far more questions than answers. That is the human condition.

I have often wondered if the Creator considered other celestial options. Imagine a flat earth and a stationary sun shining down from above, with only the variation of transient cloud cover. Life would be bright and the atmosphere always warm. But then we would not see the stars. We would miss all that the night sky affords. More importantly, we would miss the opportunity of starting life all over again in a regular diurnal cycle of variation. So every sunrise should remind us not only of faithful Providence, but also of new opportunity and a clean slate. Every sunset should remind us of the brevity of life and the mere transience of proud mankind.

But in our generation, the explosion of knowledge and the advancement of science and technology have given us new perspectives on the big questions of teleology. Astronauts and cosmonauts have looked back at the global village from space and shared their breathtaking views with all the world. It is the triumph of human genius and courage to have gained both perspectives on the human condition. Looking up from the flat earth, we feel central, big and so important. Looking down at the global earth, we feel remote, small and insignificant.

And yet the questions that arise remain the same. Those questions originate from within, even more so than from without. It is characteristic of the human spirit to seek meaning and purpose. You want your choices to count, your achievements to remain and your kind deeds to be rewarded. You appeal to others for understanding and patience, for respect and trust. You love, you judge and are judged; you honor and you cherish. You approve things that are excellent. You feel real guilt when conscience disapproves even of thought, much less of behavior. And you are forced to live with yourself day by day. You are constrained from within.

Consider the two phases in *The Evolution of* **YES!** that we've already looked at.

First, we addressed the person who was stuck in the old "*No! I Can't*" mode; the person who was practically paralyzed with negativity and pessimism. His or her head and heart were still buried in the swamp. Hopefully, you are well out of there. If not, you ought to go back and take hold of some truth or affirmation that you can hang on to and pull away. You can, if and only if you think you can.

Then we described the person who was trapped in the role of spectator, who was so busy watching that there was no time or initiative to get off the couch, or to get out of the stands, to do something that created a personal moment of fulfillment and glory. Be careful that even in reading through this book you don't stand back and think it all describes "*anybody else but me*". Rather, be alert to see yourself on every page and then take steps to connect and make real progress. Participate in the journey as we go along.

Both of those phases are important, but now we need to move along to a third type of individual--the one who says "*I should ... I really should.*"

These people know that there is something in them waiting for expression and something out there for them waiting to be experienced, but somehow they never seem to get any further than "*I should.*" It is a cosmic conclusion that pierces the heart like a personal gamma ray dispatched with ultrafine precision.   But its effect is to somehow simultaneously mobilize the mind and yet paralyze the body.

As I thought about how universal this phenomenon is ... I wondered why "*should*" had become such a huge snare, a colossal trap. Why did so many people stop at "*I should ...* " and never move any further?

"*Should*" is an emotionally loaded word that for many people is full of negative connotations. Those same people often do not realize the power in the word "*should*". It is a word intimately connected to conscience. Conscience is the place where you really and truly look after yourself. It is the nerve center where you reference and control your life. So the loss of the positive influence of an active conscience can take a serious toll on the capacity to live **YES!**

There is a real irony in our modern technological culture.

Think of the contemporary home or workplace. Observe all the modern labor-saving devices, machines, computers and robots. We now have so much gadgetry at our disposal. We hardly need to mention the automobile, jet engines, the telephone and so on. Utilities are everywhere.

Technology freed us from hard manual labor. It created extra free time. But then, having taken care of our "needs", it created in us a series of bolder and bigger "wants". Now we want what we know other people have. Enter consumerism. Enter advertising and promotion. Enter display packaging. Enter huge shopping malls with department stores and ubiquitous sensory deprivation. Enter instant gratification.

Ironically though, technology also is largely responsible for producing a society of passive spectators, diverted from doing anything concrete about satisfying our new "wants". We want to inherit the good life quickly, easily and without cost. At least judging by common behavior, we want more leisure and vacation, more service and entertainment. In fact, technology distracts us from performing the actions that are required to satisfy the very "wants" created by technology. And therein lies a paradox, if not *the* paradox, of our technological culture.

Modern generations of youth, growing up in a fast-paced, automated and relatively affluent culture seem to have believed, if anything, that they *should not* have to work so hard. They *should not* have to wait for anything. They *should not* have to persist to achieve. Success is so often taken for granted, as if it were some inalienable right of inheritance from without and from before.

That reminds me of the typical person, sometimes approaching double doors in anticipation of having them automatically swing open. They *should not* have to push or pull open any doors. Or in my travels, I observe people fretting and complaining because there is no moving walkway or escalator, or no elevator in a two-storey concourse. They *should not* have to walk a few yards, or climb up or down a flight of stairs. More seriously, many young people conclude that they *should not* have to stay in school so long. We *should not* have to pay taxes or have unwanted babies. The innocent *should not* suffer. It *should not* snow in April.

It is easy to indulge the *"should nots."* They seem to focus on rights, real and imagined, rather than on responsibilities. *"Shoulds"* on the other hand would emphasize those responsibilities, be they intrinsic or imposed.

So, it is really no surprise that people avoid the *"shoulds"* like the plague. Moreover, many *"shoulds"* do not originate in their conscience, as a witness of the things that will truly nurture them. Rather, their *"shoulds"* are often externally imposed, and in being imposed they are therefore resisted. Consequently, before we get to the life-giving part of *"I should"* we have to understand and transcend the negative aspect of this proposition--the part that drags us down. It is the very thing that seems to frustrate us so.

FRUSTRATED BY "SHOULDS"

Are you haunted by what you don't have? Do you carry around a residual idea that you ought to be doing a lot better? Do you look around you and think that life has a lot more to offer than you have experienced? Are you haunted by what you *should* have, or what you *should* do, or what you *should* be? Is there a huge gap between your reality and what you think it *should* be?

If you answered yes to any of these questions, it's time to look at *"should"* up close. First, you need to stop torturing yourself with the expectations of other people. And then, you will want to get all there is out of the magic of *"should"*. The idea really packs a punch. Too many people have 'thrown out the baby with the bath water,' when it comes to understanding the "*shoulds*" of life.

Contemporary culture finds any sense of authority or responsibility confining and restricting. We have glamorized freedom without limits. The baby boomers who control so many of the instruments that shape the culture today are products of the co-called *Sixties Revolution*. And what a revolution that was.

Moral and political objection to the Vietnam War was accompanied by an assertiveness from a generation of youth. Professor Timothy Leary led the drug culture, while Hugh Hefner led the liberal sex revolution and introduced soft porn to the mainstream. Mohammed Ali dared to resist the Vietnam draft because he could not fight other people of color, or support the cause in good conscience and without reason. The sixties gave us the Beatles who, in their search for meaning, almost legitimized the Maharishi Yogi. And then came the Rolling Stones, who also became musical icons even though they could 'get no satisfaction'. They were all rebels.

Here was a generation rejecting authority, all legalized morality and deference for anything sacred. More conservative trends rejected limitations to technical capability and dared to put a man on the moon. Elsewhere, educators rejected the 3 'R's to experiment on liberal education schemes without values education. Family definitions and roles were broken down to favor the redefinitions, to champion children's rights and to facilitate divorce. The Women's Movement erupted to blur the lines of sexual distinction from the bedroom to the boardroom.

That was a major revolutionary era.

On the bottom line it could be paraphrased simply, "Who else but me is to determine what I *should* do? Who cares? I'll do as I want". There was the triumph of individualism, the birth of the 'me' generation. But it was also the damning paradox for more than one generation. Since there is no freedom without form, there is no "I can" without "*I should*".

Maybe you're like some people I've met who physically bristle if someone says they *should* do anything. Do you relate to children of domineering parents who tried to impose their will with false moral authority? Do you wince because others dare to tell you what you *should* do?

I want to put "*should*" in clearer perspective by looking at the idea from different angles. Like so many, you are probably being pulled in a hundred different directions by the "*shoulds*" in your life. That is the reason why it's worthwhile to really come to terms, to generate some peace with them.

Let's start by looking at the "*shoulds*" that come to you through impersonal sources like television, newspapers, books, magazines, videos, the Internet and the movie screen. These I call the "*shoulds*" **outside** you. They are sufficiently removed that you can easily dismiss them, if you choose.

Then we can look at the "*shoulds*" that come from your wife or husband, parents, bosses, coaches, teachers, neighbors and friends, etc. These I call the "*shoulds*" **beside** you. They are close to home.

Finally, we'll hit paydirt, and look at the "*shoulds*" that come from you. These are the "*shoulds*" **inside** you.

"Shoulds" *Outside* **You**

The chances are good that you are continually exposed to a tremendous barrage of images, ideas and illustrations from the mass media that subtly create in you a host of expectations, both small and great. And it is these expectations which by and large may be responsible for driving you somewhat crazy, as you slavishly invest your time and energy in things and in people, causing you to behave in ways that are foreign to your true desires.

This is a bad side of "*should*." We get absorbed in being politically correct. Do you? Do you take your cues from what you see on the big screen? Do you judge appearance according to an ideal established by high fashion magazines? Do you even define yourself by the value and size of your toys which of course, you know you *should* have. Do you champion the causes that are promoted to you as if they were inherently sacred, from animal rights to rain forests, while disregarding others that are neglected such as unfair trading practices or support for single parents.

Single Parents? That brings to mind a good example in the story of Pat Kelly. She is a mother of six who spends her time talking to high school students about chastity.

Pat has spoken to tens of thousands of teenagers across North America. She knows that the sexual activity of typical teenagers is a direct function of the way sex is portrayed in popular culture. Sexually active teenagers are deeply influenced by popular statements like: "It is perfectly normal for teenagers to be sexually active and to try to prevent it is pointless." Teenagers get the point. They tell themselves: "If I am not sexually active, then I am not normal!" That's called peer pressure. Sometimes it's really heavy peer pressure, especially up close. Kids feel obliged, they *should* conform, they *should* follow the crowd. Not necessarily because they themselves really want to, but because others think they *should*.

But Pat's unique skill is helping teenagers move past all that. She gives them a second option--chastity--and tells them that it is perfectly normal and healthy to put off sexual activity until later on in life. She encourages teenagers to detach themselves from the undercurrents of popular culture and to get in touch with their true feelings about sexuality. She helps them see that they *should* wait in their own best interest. The emotional, moral, psychological, medical and social arguments all concur with that fact, but they must still personally accept it. They *should* wait.

License has led to bondage, not freedom. Pleasure has given way to pain, not prowess. Acceptance has led to rejection, not bonding. Love has led to lust, not romance. But our pop culture still says you *should* do it. 'Get the experience. Enjoy the brief thrills while you can.'

The United States leads the western world in teenage pregnancies. It was just reported that up to 14% of all girls between the ages of 15-19 had become pregnant. This was twice the rate of the next country in line, the United Kingdom, with a rate of 7%. These are astronomical figures when you consider the social implications for the next generation. No wonder it has attracted the attention and policies from the White House and Congress.

But the battle is being fought and won locally. It is a crisis of ethics and behavior, right down to the individual level. Sex education needs more than education and certainly more than sex. More condom headlines and free birth control pills in schools could never solve this problem. The culture needs an ethic and the children need both example and precepts.

As Pat will tell you ... thousands of teenagers are embracing the idea of chastity like a boat finding shelter in a brutal storm. A similar program has been sweeping across North American schools and college campuses with hundreds of thousands of youth making a public stand and committing to wait for sex within marriage. Josh McDowell and the

Campus Crusade Ministries have made a major impact with this "WHY WAIT" campaign.

It is the "outside *shoulds*" that can make life miserable. These are the "*shoulds*" that come when you are indirectly pressured to accept the prevailing precepts of modern culture, even when they run contrary to your own deepest feelings. Teenagers are not alone. That is just the stage for really acting up and acting out, when the outside pressures to conform become their biggest enemy. But all of us are subjected to these pressures. I'm sure you are too.

I specifically choose to call these the "*shoulds outside you*". They must be critically weighed and analyzed. You can screen each one with your better judgment and thus assert your identity and resist dehumanization. You need to be aware of how powerful they are in setting up the expectations that you have created for your own life.

"Shoulds" *Beside* You

I meet people everywhere who live their life with a sense of big gaps. They fall forever short. They are haunted by the things they don't have, that modern culture says they *should* have. They are haunted by what they haven't accomplished, that modern culture says they *should* have done. And they are haunted by the thought of how far their life is from the proposed ideal that they so often see portrayed, at least in theory, if not in reality. It can be painful.

Yes, modern culture precipitates many of the "*shoulds*" that give us a vague haunted feeling that we are being left behind, that something is missing, that we somehow just don't measure up. But it is by no means the only influence contributing to the phenomenon. The significant others in our life also have a lot to say about what we *should* and should not do. And the results can be catastrophic.

Here is a short exercise that will give you an opportunity to see how the "*shoulds*" of people *beside* you, like your family and close friends, have influenced your decisions. On a piece of paper, jot down some of the essential circumstances of your life. Think of your marital status, children if any, where you live, your home, your career choice, your job description, your hobbies and so on. A short list will do. Now reflect for a moment on each circumstance and the factors that influenced the decisions you made in creating those circumstances. Were they influenced by the immediate people around you? Indeed, other people have strong feelings about what you *should* do. And these people feel just as strongly that they *should* inform you frequently, and in no uncertain terms, of what you *should* do. It is their prerogative . At least, so they think and you cannot just dismiss them lightly.

This simple exercise sure takes much soulful honesty. When you pause to reflect on how much other people influence your decision-making and your life, it is amazing to find that you really do a lot of things simply because other people think you *should*.

That makes more sense earlier in life when as a child or young adult, you could benefit from the experience and perception of more seasoned veterans. But with maturity, each of us must assume more independence and responsibility. You and I must gain a knowledge of ourselves and discover our unique place in the world and what things in it can best serve us. Then we become more self-reliant and we are constrained from within. We then do what *we* know we *should*.

FUELLED BY "SHOULD"

Good biographies make the most interesting reading. It is always fascinating to learn not just the details of outstanding and meaningful lives, but the values of each celebrated individual and the motivation that caused them to do the things they did. It is clear that most if not all great achievement originates from deep conviction. Whatever such people chose to do, they were all persuaded that there was purpose and meaning to their efforts and it was their duty to follow through.

I can think of no better illustration than that of a celebrated saint of modern times. Mother Theresa won the

Nobel prize for her untiring sacrificial work among the very poor slum-dwellers of India, particularly in Calcutta. But a recent report of her hospitalization was broadcast on CNN for all the world to see. She was admitted to hospital, now in her eighties, with three life-threatening conditions. She had malaria, pneumonia and severe coronary artery disease. She was put in intensive care and then on life support. The world prayed and waited to learn of her prognosis.

With outstanding medical management and more, she was able to pull through. Days after extubation, she inquired of her doctors when she would be released from the hospital. The staff advised on Thursday morning that if all went well, she would probably go home on the weekend or early the following week. Mother Theresa was adamant. In her desperate state, against medical advice, she insisted on going home that day because ... now don't miss it ..."

"I HAVE WORK TO DO!"

Wow! Who could imagine? A message for the whole world to hear. From CNN, no less. But did they get the message? That was *passion* speaking. A passion for life, a passion for others, a passion for service. Mother Theresa knew what she *should* be doing and even in her twilight days, she felt constrained within. The fuel burned within her mind and soul. She could do no other. That should qualify her as a saint as much as all the charity work itself. It is a reflection of conscience and character. It is one thing to do a noble work, but something more to put out a noble effort, born of noble constraint. The results speak for themselves.

What about you? Do you have a work to do?

Traditionally, the normal work or job that people did was called their *vocation*. This English word derives from the Latin root *vocatio* which means 'a calling', or it may be traced further to *vocare* (to call) or even *vox* (a voice). The implication obviously was that the occupation, trade or profession that one did was, in principle, a response to a call or summons. One had an impulsion from within to perform a certain function or enter a certain career. This had religious overtones (or undertones, perhaps). There was a sense that one believed himself or herself to be called to a given task. We even developed '*vocational* schools' to teach and train young people for their specific vocations.

But it is not surprising that this terminology has all but become obsolete. Society in general has shifted its fundamental presuppositions, so that in the area of life choices and careers, everything is seen in pragmatic or utilitarian terms. No wonder guidance counselors today have such sophisticated but frustrated methodologies for their craft. They look at market forces and demographic trends more than they appeal to the *passion within*. Young people are more likely to think of job opportunities, remuneration and security, than they are to do soul-searching or to pray. Many a student today is being disillusioned by the negative projections of job prospects and the uncertain economic prognoses being dispensed in the daily media diet. Imagine being part of a so-called X-generation.

There is a major problem. You cannot look outside for the motivation to act. You cannot look around for a mission to fulfill until you first look within for a moral passion to release. You need vocation. A call from within.

"Shoulds" *Inside* You

This generation like every other, must find itself and its future in the discovery of a desire within, to have, to do and to be the best that is possible in each individual case. One by one, young people as well as displaced adults, must attune their ears to hear the resonant sounds of a voice within, calling them to achievement, to service and to duty. Like all the early explorers, pioneers, missionaries, leaders, researchers, innovators, and the like, they must rediscover in this their day, a sense of true *vocation*. They must find within a call, a tug, a push, a fire that will prompt new initiative and commitment. Then "X" - will become ex-cellence.

Do *you* share that 'passion for excellence'?

There is a similar yet contradictory word in the language which is still sometimes used to describe one's regular work. It is the word *avocation*, derived from the Latin also: *a-(or ab-)* meaning 'away' and again *vocare* (to call). This word implies 'a calling away'. It is more precise then, to use it to describe something one does *in addition to* his or her vocation or work. More particularly, it suggests an activity one does more for pleasure, like a hobby, or something of lesser importance.

Could I suggest that the only basis for an *avocation* is to first have a *vocation*. It is as if one applies oneself with such diligence, because of a sense of calling and duty, that to engage in something else for just money, or mere pleasure or simply to pass time, they must be called *away from* their station. You could hardly enjoy or even appreciate an *avocation* without a *vocation*. But we have missed the call of both in recent times.

"*Should*" is an inner urge. It is the truest and highest, if not the only, valid motivation for the decisions we make and the way we choose to live. With the passion and fire of inner conviction, there is no task too burdensome, no duty too demanding and no obstacle insurmountable. Fueled by mere "*should*", heroes have walked into bullets, been burnt at the stake, scaled mountain peaks, survived decades in prison, sacrificed careers for kids, evangelized savage tribes, survived deprivation and disease in slums, labored in isolation, loved the unlovable, and much more. In the same way, ordinary folk have simply done a good day's work, given of their best, responded to challenge, cared for the needy, assumed responsibility, and so on, all because they felt they "*should*".

When all is said and done, there is no substitute

anywhere for the conscience, the conviction, the passion that allows you to know what you *should* do, and then constrains you to do it. Yet you must go beyond the mere fascination of "*should,* " beyond the frustration that you do experience from all those 'outside' and 'beside' you who continue to impose their "*shoulds*" on you. You must discover the fuel of passion and conviction *inside* you that will move you, not just to feel or to wish, but to act.

The universe may not be unfolding as it *should*, but at least, *you* can. You can respond to the call from above and beyond, the one that filters through that still small voice within. You really *should*.

"*I should*" is still a long way from the unequivocal **'YES!'** But you are moving along. You are slowly getting there. So continue. Listen to yourself and be prepared to take a *risk*. You cannot stop now. It's a price you have to pay. You will soon discover that it's worth it.

* * *

The Evolution of **YES!** *unfolds:*

You

must

participate!

4

Risk

("If ... ")

As we trace this evolutionary process to **YES!**, we find ourselves emerging from the dark, foreboding abyss of negativity and pessimism of Phase One. There we saw how poor self-image will paralyze the sad individual so that they attempt nothing, because they simply believe the lie *"No, I can't"*. In Phase Two we went beyond the posture of the idle spectator who thinks that passion and productivity must always be the right of someone else. We substituted *'anybody else but me'* with *'anybody, including me'*. In Phase Three we underscored that there is within each of us an irresistible urge to do what we know *we should*. Yes, there is a constraining ethic, a vocation, otherwise an avocation if you please, that prompts action and propels change and growth.

This brings us now to a point of reflection: a question of risk. It cannot be avoided on any path to affirmative living. Life itself is conditional.

LIFE IS CONDITIONAL

Are you indulging in the things you really love to *do* on a regular basis? What about the things you would love to *have* and more importantly, the person you would like to *be*? Are you enjoying *la joie de vivre* right now ... today ... at this particular stage or phase of life ... or even life per se? Life in the affirmative present is full of passion and excitement. We are daily summoned to experience a thrilling adventure. Are you responding to such a call as you step out each morning? When you face the sunrise, you alone must monitor your *triple-E index*: Enthusiasm, Excitement and Exhilaration.

Being totally honest with yourself, are you getting everything out of your career and family life that a person with your education, skills, experience, and ambition should be getting? Or are you getting less? Perhaps you are accepting less than you 'should' because some condition has not been met and you are unwilling to take a chance. You would not *dare* ... to win. That's what this Phase is all about.

So many people settle for so much less than their skills and experience suggest they are capable of having. Do you? When you look at your own situation, is there a gap between where you are now and where you reasonably think you could be, given all the things you have going for you?

There is a natural and healthy dissatisfaction with self that prompts growth and initiates change. Complacency is no virtue. We choose to grow because we burst at the seams of past experience with the eager anticipation and desire for what we could *have*, what we could *do*, and what we could *be*. Does that include you? If not, why not?

For many of you reading this now, the chances are that whatever may be holding you back starts with a big ... "IF ... " Your mind could be constrained, your spirit confined and your future controlled by the awesome weight of this little but big, two-letter word. This explosive word is the spark-plug of the conditional life. It ignites a subset of pre-conditions and post-conditions that can incapacitate you and leave you in a state of suspended animation.

Imagine a baseball player eager to steal a base. He gingerly steps off first base, getting a lead as he straddles the line in a crouched posture. With his palms outstretched, his torso arched with precision and his slender legs tap dancing on the turf, he eyes the minute detail of the pitcher's movement as he goes through the evolution of a delivery to the plate. He knows exactly what he would like to do. *If* he could get a jump ... *if* the pitcher will follow through to the catcher ... *if* he has the speed ... *if* the catcher has a poor arm, or at least delivers a poor throw ... *if* the infield plays back ... *if* the shortstop or second baseman is napping ... *if* ... *if* ... *if* ... a list of **pre-conditions**. He would attempt a steal now *if* he could complete his patented slide into second ... or better yet, *if* the hitter could connect in a 'hit-and-run' play ... *if* getting into scoring position was guaranteed to set up another run ... *if* he does not get thrown out ... *if* the catcher overthrows to the bag ... another set of **post-conditions**. But the question remains, will he run on this delivery? Only he knows. He must take that risk. He will never get to second base with his foot on first. That's for sure.

For lots of people, before they get to the point where **YES!** is their overwhelming response to life, a big stack of "IF's" have to be dealt with first. They fall asleep at first base waiting for conditions to be perfect before they make a dash for the bag at second. Are *you* still on first?

Or consider this: "The only way to pick some of the best fruit is to go out on a limb." Some people are content to endure the cheap fruits of their labor because they dare not risk taking a chance on their future. They want the best of life served to them on a platter. But that is not how the best of life is served. You must reach out, You must extend yourself. You must risk to reap the best of life.

The path to innovation is laid down on the shoulders of those brave men and women who dared to stick their necks out to peer where no one else had looked. You will never see beyond the ordinary horizons of your own life unless you dare to stretch and strain to gain periscopic vision that sees over the skyline. This is the path of big discovery. Ask any researcher, inventor or explorer. From Michael Faraday stepping inside his super charged electrostatic cage, to Dr. Jonas Salk injecting himself with his own polio vaccine, or to Neil Armstrong taking 'one small (*precarious*) leap for man but one giant (*presumptuous*) step for mankind.'

When all is said and done, you must take a leap of faith by believing in yourself, believing in latent possibility and believing in the future. You must *dare* ... to win! Or as Les Brown put it, *'It isn't over until you win.'* But you must play.

LIFE IS RISKY

"IF" is a limiting condition that only confines and constrains the human spirit. It is the switch that often turns out the light and turns off the heat that would otherwise ignite and fuel human creativity and potential. It is so unwise and unproductive to impose both pre- and post- conditions before you venture into the unknown.

To live **YES!** you must be prepared for risk. The *"IF"* problem is actually a risk problem. Life is risky. To get anywhere in life, it usually becomes necessary at some time or other, to take some risks. Naturally the risks make us feel pretty apprehensive and nervous, so we do what we can to avoid them. But there does not seem to be any way around them. Or is there?

If you have ever spent some time with a financial planner, or investigated the financial markets, you will be familiar with the idea of a risk/return ratio. The idea is simple: the lower the risk, the lower the potential return. When we are talking about financial securities, the ones with the lowest risks (like government bonds) also carry the lowest returns. If you want to generate higher returns, you have to consider investment with higher levels of risk. Risk and return go hand in hand.

In medicine there is a different kind of ratio, classically known as the risk/benefit ratio. This governs the intervention by any wise physician, or more importantly any competent surgeon. The application of any test, drug, radiation therapy, chemotherapy or surgical procedure incurs at least a finite risk of harm. It could be mild harm, with common symptoms like nausea, diarrhea, urticaria (rash), dizziness, insomnia or the like. Or in the extreme, the side effects or consequences could be paralysis, other serious misadventure or even death. Some consequences are called idiosyncratic because they arise without any explanation.

All good doctors must assess the risk/benefit ratio before prescribing any therapeutic or surgical intervention. They must assess and advise the patient of the risk associated with an indicated course of action, and then balance that risk against the potential benefit to the patient. The only justification for high risk intervention is overwhelming potential benefit in the absence of any lower-risk alternative. That is the intent of the Hippocratic oath: (above all) to *'do no harm.'* Unless this is done clearly and carefully, the patient's best interest is not served. That exposes the patient to potential harm and exposes the physician to possible legal claim.

But the commonplace *"IF'"* is different. Most commonly, *"IF"* precedes a set of unsatisfied conditions that focus on the risk involved in a new, different or proactive course of action that we hesitate to follow. We use it as a hinge to close the door to initiative, innovation and ingenuity.

In a way ... "IF" says *'I'd love to get the return but I have no interest in assuming that much risk'*. If you hear and examine enough "If only ... " statements, you begin to see that they are all a variation on the same theme: "If only I could be rewarded without having to assume any risk." That is asking for an experience of the good life by the cheap way. It is seeking something for nothing. But more importantly, it is choking off the potential for personal growth as character muscles are flexed.

Life is in reality a series of risks and rewards, a true balancing act. When you concentrate your efforts on trying to detach one from the other you end up pretty frustrated. Consider each of the following in turn and assess the potential for risk involved in each case:

1. Going into space,
2. Flying across the ocean,
3. Driving to work,
4. Stepping off the curb,
5. Taking an elevator,
6. Standing on the balcony,
7. Remaining indoors,
8. Turning on the stove,

9. Getting out of bed,

10. Staying alive...

Did you get the point? Accidents do happen. It's a sliding scale. These are all risky adventures. The magnitude may decrease but there is no way to escape the finite risk of life and still get a reward. If you seek to minimize risk, you must crawl back into a shell, become introverted, vegetate, and finally, you will still *risk* ultimate implosion that can destroy life itself. That would be sheer folly.

LIFE IS BALANCED

The Art of Life is balance. A lot of the good things in life come in polar extremes and by concentrating totally on one or the other, you will miss some of what life has to offer.

The ancient philosophers perceived this simple truth and underlined the concept of duality in nature: light and dark, hot and cold, earth and sky, fire and water, male and female, etc. More modern philosophers would describe positive and negative, matter and antimatter, wave and particle, entropy and enthalpy, free will and determinism, time and space, etc.

Any adequate perspective of the world, ancient or modern, must do justice to this ambivalence, this two-sided reality. Just as we need two eyes to give clear visual depth perception or two ears to scan the environment of sound, so we need to examine the polar extremes of the reality called life to perceive the depth and height of which we are capable in daily experience.

More simply, if we imagine that life is like a teeter-totter, the good news is that we find *good* things at both ends. Life is lived to its fullest when we include them both and so keep the teeter-totter in balance. The consideration, time and effort taken to balance our competing needs that seem to be in opposition, really pays big dividends in the end.

What are some of these competing needs and how do we keep them in balance?

Many people struggle to balance the extremes of security versus opportunity. Here is one of the classic trade-offs that you have to continually come to terms with. Opportunity can be one part of life that really makes living worthwhile. It relates to life under an open sky. You can soar, you can roam. You look into the face of eternity and flap your wings like a free-spirited eagle. You are uninhibited, leaving roots and walls behind. But that leaves no space to call one's home and no surety to call one's own.

Some people see opportunity everywhere. They never run out of new and challenging goals to work at and to conquer. And they never need to know answers to everything because they never need an anchor.

Yet there are others who have a difficult time embracing opportunity because it seems like a direct challenge to their feelings of security. They love when things are predictable. That way they can plan, they can prepare, they can position themselves for the future. They are protected from impulsiveness and spared much anxiety. They know their bottom line and accept that they can cope with it. No storms rage, no tension builds, no drama unfolds on their stage. They only know the serene life where things remain calm and quiet, stable and secure. The sense of danger they experience at breaching such feelings of security almost paralyses them into maintaining the status quo.

How do you successfully balance your need for security with your need to pursue a special opportunity that is the virtual fulfillment of your dreams? How do you manage to break through the wall of attachment to security? How do you strike a balance? What separates the people who take a chance on their dreams, from the people who stay put and spend the rest of their professional lives singing the refrain ..."If only I had ... "?

Like so many things in life, it all comes down to a matter of *choice*. In the end, you simply decide for or against the status quo.

But from whom do you take your counsel? What influence dominates your will?

If fear of the unknown governs your decision, there is no question which choice you will make. Irrational fear is the enemy of opportunity. Almost every opportunity carries with it a fear of failure; a feeling of fear that can begin to erode any and all feelings of security. But fear and opportunity are two sides of the same coin--you can't have one without the other.

You must therefore transcend your irrational fears after the relative facts have been carefully gathered and deemed to be net positive. Collecting more facts does not make the fear go away. It is important to calculate what you can, yes, but what you cannot ... you risk. Susan Jeffers made a clear point in the title of her fine book: *"Feel the Fear and Do It Anyway."* You can't wait for the fear to go away before you make a decision ... you could be waiting forever. In order to take advantage of opportunity when it comes knocking ... healthy self-confidence is a must.

For many people life can be an overwhelming experience. They see all around them evidence to conclude that life is often brutal. So they harbor in the dark corners of their mind the thought that they might be subjected to some of that brutality in the future, unless they carefully manage their affairs with maximum caution. They are paranoid. They think the future holds some potentially scary things, and to ward them off they must always play it safe. They want to create a future that they can manage. They want no surprises and no great challenges.

But the future doesn't have to be that scary. No matter how everything turns out ... you must feel that you can handle it. Don't be naive enough to imagine that life will progress without any bumps or rough patches. Of course it won't. You must assert a quiet confidence that even if life does present a couple of twists and turns, you will do just fine. At least, you will survive. That is a powerful thought that can really help you open the door to opportunity. No matter what happens ... you will handle it. All your decisions need not turn out to be correct. Even if some are wrong, you can be confident that you will cope with whatever life has in store.

To the extent that you remove irrational fear from your mind, and to the extent that you maintain a quiet confidence in your ability to handle whatever the future holds, to that extent you are poised to take advantage of the opportunities that life presents.

After all, life is a series of balancing acts. You have to find your own place in the never-ending trade-offs between opposing ideas. There are lots of them. When it comes to earning a living, do you gravitate towards brain or brawn? Are you attracted by stability or change? Do you want to be involved with a small business or a large corporation? Are you more comfortable alone, or are you a socializer? Do you gravitate towards creative work or are you more comfortable in routine tasks? Are you interested in image, or does income mean more to you? Do you thrive on immediate gratification, or are you more attracted to long term investments? Are you interested in getting a business that involves the whole family, or would you be happier in the more traditional role?

The answers to each of these questions form a continuum, from one extreme to the next. You do have your own choice spot on the continuum. When you impose a conditional "*IF* ..." you are telling yourself that there is a place that you would rather be than where you are now. That is psychologically and emotionally unhealthy.

But you need to find your own comfort zone, a homebase, a place where there is no need at all to say ... "*If only* ... " In that way, wherever you are, you can be truly there.

Risk is a part of life, and the sooner you can incorporate a healthy attitude toward risk into your life, the more joy and prosperity you are going to experience.

Could you still be only ***dreaming***? That is a poor substitute for the effective use of your imagination ... Wake up. It's time to stop dreaming.

* * *

The Evolution of **YES!** *unfolds:*

You must

risk

participation!

5

Dreaming

("I would like to")

CHILDHOOD DREAMING

If you think back to your childhood years, I am sure you would fondly remember the magical times of wishing upon a star, or throwing a couple coins over your shoulder as you made a secret wish. You probably shared in the breaking of the chicken wish bone at the dinner table to see if your wish or someone else's would come true. At Christmas and even other less eventful dates on the calendar, we all had wish lists. And let's face it, to this day we blow out the candles on our birthday cake ... yes, after making a wish.

All this "wish-making" was and is, a lot of harmless fun. But in fact, more than just harmless fun, wishful thinking is closely linked to a fundamental human need. You and I need hope, the promise of a pleasant or desirable future, the prospect of something better to come. You need hope that your economic situation will improve, that your health will be good and that your job will be secure. You need to trust that peace will prevail, that you will experience true love and that your relationships will grow. You need to believe that your dreams will be realized and much, much more. Sometimes the only thing that gives you the strength to carry on is the hope that things will get better and that the storms of life will pass.

After all, the promise of the future is an awesome, compelling force. It fortifies the human will and stretches your resilience beyond normal limits. It births the extraordinary. Where hope dies, the will to transcend your difficulties and pursue your dreams dies with it. So you need to hope, because this expectation is one of the sweetest gifts of life and one of the real joys of living.

But should you not be selective in how and why you dream, in what you anticipate, in how you prepare for what is to come and in what you place your hope? Of course.

We all should admire wishful thinking and encourage this quality in children. They have the right to imagine the future that they would ideally choose for themselves. They can make as many wishes as they like and live lives of pure, innocent fantasy. But let's ask the big question.

Why do children like to wish upon a star? Why is the innocent wishful thinking of children such a powerful influence on their young minds?

The answer is pretty obvious. Children like to dream and wish because they have no real power to alter their lives in any meaningful way. Children do not have the luxury of picking their parents, or choosing their brothers or sisters. They are not asked to select their teacher or their school. They have no means to purchase their own toys, much less put a swimming pool in the backyard or fly around the world. Therefore, they believe in magic and Santa Claus, in a friendly Mickey Mouse and superaction heroes. They are at home on Sesame Street. And they do have guardian angels. In their world, where the imaginary blurs into reality and vice versa, things are as they would choose. All is fair in love, war and the mind of a child. It's all like magic.

Without any real power, children rely on the magical power of dreams and wishes to express their deepest desires. Rather than packing up their suitcase, calling a taxi, and heading out into the world, the average five year old retreats into a private but personal world of wishful thinking. It is a world where he or she can call the shots. There are no limitations. Everything is possible because there is no one there to say 'NO!'. No one to say 'STOP!'. Children understandably feel subjected to random forces completely outside their own control, and in the face of that arbitrary power which makes them helpless, they concoct an inner dreamscape that they do control. It is powered by the limitless energy of simple wishful thinking. This is all a completely innocent habit that is one of the special joys of childhood. It is rich in benefits and devoid of risk.

Oh the joys, of childhood! Kids have no responsibility and so little reality to restrain their fantasy. There are no dark compelling memories to inhibit their amazing potential to conquer their worst fear. They rule their world. It is probably an inalienable right. What do you think?

But now you can ask yourself a bigger question, without being a killjoy. When this harmless diversion of the normal child is carried over into adulthood in a magnified way, is that not potentially harmful?

A typical child, with a normal psychological make-up will, over time, begin to outgrow the magical thinking that characterizes the childhood dreamer. Magical thinking begins to recede as the child develops more and more control over his or her own environment. When a child begins to see the world as a place of cause and effect, when actions begin to produce desirable or undesirable results, when a child begins to exercise a choice over simple things like meals and wardrobe, then the need for magical thinking dwindles. Fantasy begins to fade. Reality sets in. There is a gradual appreciation for the value of Law and the law of Value. A child sees that life is an equation ... *you get out of life what you put into it.* Action produces results. As you make up (or not make up) your bed, so you lie in it. This process is just one of the many developmental passages that the average child goes through on the path to mature adulthood.

ADULT DREAMING

But let's face it ... not every child makes it through that passage. There is an unbelievable amount of evidence that the magical thinking of the powerless child is alive and well in a disturbing number of adults who never managed to outgrow it. They fail to take control, to assume ultimate responsibility for their own thinking and behavior. They want to win or inherit their destiny. Rather than flap their wings, they wait for a strong wind to lift them above the undesirable circumstances of their present existence. The evidence is overwhelming. It is a major hurdle along the evolutionary path to **YES!**

Let me illustrate.

National, state and city lotteries have grown to ridiculous proportions. It is a testament to human greed and vanity that almost everyone wants to get lucky. It makes headline news whenever some poor unfortunate person somewhere in obscurity has their world shattered in this ridiculous fashion.

A recent winner chose to wait for quite some time before claiming his winnings even though he was sure of his largesse. When questioned, he claimed that he wanted to relish the joy of *anticipation* ... for as long as possible. He was probably wise. Those were the last days of his *real* life. He graduated to emotional and personal oblivion. Pity, I say.

Then there is that common seniors' pastime called Bingo. It's almost like a religion in some circles. Why sit at tables and play a game of brainless luck and chance, with little interpersonal interaction, no skills, no humor, no variety, no personality, nothing but gambling with the ridiculous hope of winning? Is this all they could find to do? We know that many folks could go to a café or lounge and socialize all they want for a quarter of what they spend at the Bingo hall. In fact, they would actually talk and share more.

The industry caters to these vulnerable souls living on fixed incomes who have no more control over their economic life. They sustain their wishful thinking by their expectation of winning one of these nights. Yet their pocket book continues to shrink. Furthermore, the pastime is addictive in a truly clinical sense. It is not social behavior, it is psychological dependency. It is an avaricious trap for the heart and mind. That is subtle but real.

Consider the book racks at the local variety store. There you find row upon row of *romance* novels that flood the booksellers' list year after year as one of the top selling lines. I am told that if you've read one, you've read them all. Change the author, change the style, change the setting of characters in time and place, but it's the same chemistry and definitely the same biology.

Modern North American society has an almost insatiable appetite for these pulp romance novels which sustain the inner dream world of the people who buy them. Where the real thing has failed, bring on the counterfeit. Enjoy in fiction what the facts of life deny. Titillate the senses with strokes of steamy lust that have neither neurons, hormones or seminal fluids. How could that ever be the real thing? It won't ever satisfy, so move on to the next one in thrilling disgust. No wonder they keep selling.

And while you are at the variety store, why not pick up the newspaper and check your horoscope to see what the stars have in store for your life over the next few days? Find out what your life holds today. Get some guidance for your important decision-making, then reshuffle your priorities and values accordingly. See what sign your lover should be, lest you make the wrong strategic move on your next date. Work on those stubborn characteristics that the stars have molded into your personality if you wish to 'win friends and influence people'. It seems like everyone is consulting the stars. Even the elite are unashamedly quoted as followers of the paranormal. It is just one more way that we reach out to the mysterious realm to explain or influence our unsatisfied lives.

If that is not enough, you can formalize the same barren philosophies with pseudoreligious jargon and even ritual, in the deceitful New Age phenomenon. Make nonsense of the sense in your life and cause reality to merge with speculative fantasy. Deny history and guilt, ignore redemption and Holy Presence and make petty fallen gods of us all. Pursue mediums and seek contact with the departed while the living shout into our ears, stare into our eyes and tug at our hearts, for love and recognition, for service and respect. But New Age is not new. Many years ago, reprobate Kings of Israel and pagan worshippers touted the same speculative ideas and practiced similar divinations. They faced the consequences. We should have learned by now.

If you get tired of reading romance novels and lottery results, of scanning the horoscope or seeking pseudo religious experience, you can always head down to the casino to generate a little excitement.

A generation ago, to visit the casino you might have had to travel far, perhaps even to Las Vegas or Atlantic City. But that's no longer necessary, because if your local community hasn't already started building a casino, the chances are good that they might be planning one right now or jealously monitoring the revenues next door. Casino gambling in North America is exploding with interest and investment.

And gambling in North America is not restricted to casinos. It was reported that the introduction and success of the new Scratch & Win gambling cards doubled the number of inquiries to Gamblers Anonymous within the first year. We can easily throw all the other inventive gambling schemes into the pile, from sweepstakes and hockey pools, to video terminals and poker machines, to prize fights and racetracks. Gambling is making a full frontal assault on the time and resources of the North American population.

These are some of the more obvious examples, but this particular way of thinking and living is pervading even the mainstream business environments. Banks routinely put together mortgage offers that include a "chance" at winning a free mortgage. Other businesses are following suit in more and more creative ways. 'Scratch & Win' for example, is big business for initiatives in marketing and promotions. It is almost routine for gas stations, car rental agencies, city hotels, restaurants, etc. to award door prizes and raffle big ticket items for random selection of guests who leave business cards or complete questionnaires. Everybody wants to win, the bigger, the better. Popular game shows on TV turn the social malaise into an acceptable form of recreation with fabulous prizes for guessing games, wheels of fortune and much more. If the price is right, you get to take home the prizes, with additional goodies.

What are we to make of this juggernaut that is rolling through North American culture? What conclusions can we draw? And what does this have to do with you living a positive, passionate and productive life characterized by **YES!**?

Throughout this century the greatest source of resistance to the gambling mentality and subculture has come from religionists. Most ethicists would agree that there is a clear moral and social component to the debate, but I want to approach it from a fresh perspective. I wonder what this exaggerated and prolonged sense of magical or wishful thinking, this "something-for-nothing" attitude, does to the level of enjoyment and satisfaction that adults get out of life. When I think of the millions who can only dream their lives away, I really do wonder. Can they live by design?

LIFE BY DESIGN

This tremendous upsurge in gambling and escapist activities really is a reflection of the general feelings of helplessness and powerlessness that many people end up feeling well into adulthood. They may not articulate it, but they are led to act as if "chance" were the only way of enjoying the best of life or meeting with any success. And the consequences are potentially devastating. Imagine what life would be like if you felt that you had no ability to "create" your own fulfillment or success, but were entirely at the mercy of mere chance?

This chapter is intended to demonstrate to the reader who wants to *win* the best of life rather than *earn* it, that when it comes to success, and more importantly satisfaction, the rules have not changed. Success still comes from inner desire or passion translated into well thought out plans which are pursued with a dogged perseverance. Success is only passion expressed. You truly do get out of life what you put into it. Action alone will produce results. All casinos, lotteries, bingos, horoscopes, sweepstakes, romance novels and all the world of wishful thinking--it all *demands* little and therefore can only *deliver* little. Nothing for nothing, that's the *real* bottom line.

But there is always good news!

You are still the Captain of your ship, with choices to make, decisions to weigh, plans to execute and accomplishments to celebrate. Instead of waiting for the stars to make you happy, count your blessings. Do something. Enter into a life of passion to make yourself feel energized and fulfilled. Instead of waiting for the lottery to make you financially successful, create ideas and associations, make investments, cultivate skills, attempt something that can afford financial gains. Instead of waiting to feel like your knight in shining armour is riding out of the pages of Harlequin, go and immerse yourself in the social life of your community and expose yourself to intimacy. Living a life by design is still the sweetest way to spend your days.

Fulfillment comes from applying your best efforts to an endeavor that is meaningful to you. And the more obstacles that you have to overcome en route to your goal, the greater the feeling of accomplishment that you will experience when you are successful.

Would you like to have a Gold Medal? Then try buying one, the biggest and best that you can find anywhere. Wear it. Sport it everywhere. Then sit and watch a real competitive event. Marvel at the intensity, the devotion, the passion that a serious athlete brings to the competition. Imagine the discipline, the strain and the pain that pushes the athlete beyond normal limits to achieve their ultimate goal. Then follow through to the Olympic awards ceremony, see the tears running down the athletes' cheeks while their national anthem is played and the crowds cheer. You would want immediately to return your purchase to whichever jeweler supplied it. Get the point?

Lottery winners don't change all that much after they win the Big One. Their character, personality, quality of inner life and mind-set remain essentially the same. Only their economics, their environs and their expectations change. In essence, the money only gave the people who won that much more opportunity to be the people that they already were. The people who were broke and destitute when they won their big jackpot, quite surprisingly, often ended up broke and destitute a few short years after collecting the money. If they had poor habits or were unproductive, if they had barren minds or experienced lonely days, if they were irresponsible, selfish, indulgent, fretful, etc., all this remained. And if you think about it, that's what you might expect. It makes perfect sense. Money by itself won't make you smarter, or more disciplined, or more resourceful. Money won't give you an intelligent plan for living, or make you a better decision maker. Money doesn't change you at all. The most it will do is to change your financial circumstances for a while.

Is this not the salient fact that those who have staked

their horse to a life of chance have completely forgotten? Even if their horse *were* to win the big Derby, which of course is overwhelmingly unlikely, the Jackpot would not solve the basic questions in life that we all tend to avoid.

What skills and resources do you have that you ought to develop? What goals are most important to you? What do you value most? What are the accomplishments in life that give you satisfaction? What meaning do you give to life and the things that occupy your time? All these questions can only be answered by living life by design, and not by default or by chance. That's the essential point.

A life by design implies taking both responsibility and control. It means that you choose to be proactive and to anticipate the results of the actions you choose to take on a consistent basis. You can write your own script and cast yourself in your own choice leading role. Then the outcome is never in doubt. In the end, you will truly win. Yes, WIN!

IMAGINATION

Now let's be perfectly clear. A life by design does not in any way limit the amount of dreaming you can do. Exploiting the power of conceiving the inconceivable and of imagining the unimaginable is a huge part of almost any successful endeavor. The power of the imagination is one of life's greatest gifts. It is a real, unfathomable power, one that you wield yourself, one that you can choose to put into service to realize your own desires and goals, and at will.

There is a big difference between imagination as a creative tool and the wishful thinking, daydreaming and hopeful (or hopeless!) gambling that we've commented on before. Most importantly, imagination is a conscious, disciplined, focused, deliberate and creative exercise. By it, you can harness all the forces of desire, all the strength of will and character, all the power of personality, all the energy of creative thought, to go beyond reason and intellect into a new world that is unseen and unknown, but nevertheless one waiting to be explored.

Imagination can bring all the psychological, mental and spiritual energy to a focal point to produce whatever you choose to conceive. Creative ideas and solutions will explode in your brain. At the same time it will ignite a fire within your bosom if you dare to hold vivid representations of the possible. This will bring your will into submission to a new idea or ideal. Therefore that makes the imagination the ultimate master of the soul. When exercised actively and consistently, it becomes the dominant influence on your mind, your heart and your will.

Mere wishful thinking encourages you to take your hands off the steering wheel of your own life. In contrast, imagination fires your passion to hold on to the controls and to drive forward to accomplish the impossible. In the world of the imagination anything is possible. You can never overestimate the resource of an unfettered imagination.

Imagination gives you focus, letting you zero in on a real and graphic picture of what you want to create. The greater the detail, the clearer the picture. Imagination creates what doesn't exist, all the while holding the picture in place until it finally does exist. At first, it exists only in your mind, unseen but no less real. It is an amazing process in which your imagination leads, and the body follows. Your dreams constrain your activities. You use your imagination to build a target that acts as your goal. It becomes the magnetic bull's eye, drawing you, pulling you up and out and giving you focus.

The greatest tragedy in the life of any mind is a dull and never used imagination. It is with your imagination that you begin to create a new paradigm, a new way of looking at the world. It is with your imagination that you set up the constants in your life. Forrest Shaklee said it simply: "What you think ... you look. What you think ... you do. What you think ... you are."

To change your life, you have to change your thinking, and to change your thinking you have to plug into the powers of your own imagination. The life you experience is to a large extent the visible expression of the life you truly imagine. You can create inventions, solutions, opportunities, relationships and so much more, first in the world of your own imagination, and then they will translate into the real world of experience that you know. If you don't use your imagination, it becomes sluggish and lethargic. The old saying, "Use it or lose it ..." has never been more true than in the case of the imagination.

Disney is right 'imagination is the preview of all life's coming attractions.' Your life simply lags behind your focused conceptions, or lack thereof. Your thoughts are the preamble that leads in to your life. Your imagination is the only self-imposed limitation on what you can become in the future.

Success always begins in exactly the same place, the imagination. Through goal setting you can turn the invisible into the visible. But that will do you no good until you have formed a clear mental picture of what you are trying to accomplish.

One of the easiest and most effective means you have of changing your life, of getting out of the rut that you may find yourself in, is through the power of the imagination. Benjamin Franklin claimed that the first thing he always did every morning was to take his imagination out for a walk. He would imagine all kinds of different scenarios as a way to energize and give vitality to his day. They didn't necessarily have to be related to the current project that he was working on. His whole idea was just to get his imagination muscles working, to stimulate the powers of his mind in order to arrive at new solutions.

Creative imagination is an entirely learned skill. You have all the basic equipment that you need to have a wonderfully vivid and creative imagination. The real challenge is how willing you are to work at developing it. Of course, it will take practice but it will be worth it.

Reflect on the following summary. Let it ignite the fire of your imagination 'til its light and heat spread throughout your being and you complete that cycle of success.

In the world of the imagination,
anything is possible.
You will never know what is possible for you
until you attempt the impossible.
When you attempt the impossible,
you will achieve at least the incredible.
When you believe the incredible,
your success will be inevitable!

All that is true, unless you choose to make *excuses*. Don't try that. Just keep on moving, excuse or no excuse.

* * *

The Evolution of **YES!** *unfolds:*

You must risk participation

as you

pursue your dream!

6

Excuses

("But ... ")

You are making solid progress. You have gained a foothold to move away from the negativism of Phase One. You have become an active participant and insist that you want a piece of the live action described in Phase Two. You got involved because you are constrained to make a difference in your life, to do what you know you ought to do. That was Phase Three. Then in Phase Four, you dared to take the risk, to open the doors of opportunity and step out in pursuit of your dream. In the previous phase we considered how wishful thinking was the antithesis of a vigorous and productive imagination. You now dare to focus creatively on what is possible for you and you probably have some new ideas.

As we continue to progress along the evolutionary path to positive, passionate and productive living, we come now to a classic Phase. Here is someone who has fired their imagination with visions of great enterprise. They even know exactly what they want. They have successfully dipped into the pool of imaginative goal setting and come up with an idea that really excites them. It is an idea that touches them in the deepest part of their being, something worth working for. They will toil and persevere and do what needs to be done to achieve the desired results. At least, in principle.

To have come this far is an accomplishment. But many a dreamer never gets a clear definition of what needs to happen next. So often incidental goal-setting that goes on beside the backyard pool or at the sixteenth hole on the golf course never gets crystallized. Some people get stuck at the talking stage. They talk the good talk, but they only talk. They paint a picture of their ultimate goal with verbal strokes that dance and ring with excitement. But they only paint. They are extraordinary dream merchants, but they never trade. They never go any further. Why is this?

If you ask such fanciful planners and entrepreneurs why they are stuck in the talking stage, or even the planning stage, their answer usually starts with a single word ... the word that is the focus of this chapter. They'll tell you that they would love to go on ... *BUT*! ... There is the inevitable excuse, the irresistible logic to cause instant paralysis. With this simple verbal hinge, massive doors of opportunity swing inward and downward to shut out the inviting possibilities of the future. Suddenly the dream comes to an abrupt end. All initiative dies. They freeze as the excuses are born.

EXCUSING EXCUSE

An excuse is not just a mere hurdle for those who fail to act. It is like Mount Everest on a windy day. That is, it becomes practically insurmountable. It is not only reasonable and necessary, to their way of thinking, but an excuse is a sufficient condition for inactivity. There is no such thing as a bad excuse, or a poor excuse. As long as they can generate a "BUT ..." these escapists and quitters justify any degree of failure. They feel relieved of all responsibility and absolved of all guilt. With a simple excuse they need say no more. Doing nothing is the obvious thing to do. So, that is exactly what they *do*. Nothing. Unfortunately, getting or achieving nothing becomes the legitimate consequence. And that is also what they *get*. Nothing. They make excuses, therefore they get no results.

Are you prone to making excuses? In some respects they are almost second nature. But it has been said that when you take away everything else from life, when you reduce it to the bottom line, when each of us has completed our journey here, we will produce only two things ... *results* and *excuses*. We will present them in reciprocal proportion to each other. That's all there is in the end. Possibly.

Before we look at some common excuses, let us take a look at the general love affair we have with excuses.

Some people are learned masters at exploiting the edges of decent society. They excel at using any excuse to dodge the bullet, to avoid the responsibility for taking care of their part of the human tapestry. All the while they imagine themselves to be so cunningly clever because they slip through one sticky situation after another. For them, making excuses tends to become an end in itself. But that is never really the end. Never.

Excuses that are made *before* action is taken, preclude any possibility of doing what truly needs to be done. Opportunity is wasted. Potential remains dormant and hope dies. Excuses that are made *after* the fact do not change the facts, neither do they negate the possibilities of what could have been. Nor do they put the conscience to rest, or inspire any necessary change. Regrets are common. Growth remains inhibited and consequences follow. Not surprising.

Excuses are never enough.

Making excuses can become a pattern of behavior that distills into a character trait which helps to define your destiny. The Gospel includes parables of those who used one excuse or another to evade responsibility, to justify sloth or indulgence and eventually to deny the truth. In every case, their end was their shame and loss.

What excuses are you prone to make? How do you try to avoid the challenge of life that you are called to face? Why may you not be where you ought to be now? Or simply, why are you not doing what you ought to do? When you have breathed your last breath, what will you have accomplished or left behind? Will you have *results* to show for your diligence, application and the sweat of your brow? Or will you have more *excuses* to offer that are flippant and vulgar? That is a choice. The decision is up to you.

EXCUSES, EXCUSES, EXCUSES

It is unnecessary to survey here the many excuses that are used as rationalizations for not getting desired results. Any list would be incomplete and far too long. But we can focus on a few common examples to gain a better sense of how they can be dissolved. As we work through these, remember that good excuses are no more productive than bad excuses. They remain nothing but excuses. Let's look at the first one. It's very common.

"I am too old."

The immediate question arises: Too old for what? "How old are you?" More specifically, what is the age of your body (calendar age)? What is the age of your mind (academic curiosity). And what is the age of your spirit (level of passion)? Hopefully, that's in declining order.

When it comes to age there is so much evidence, both positive and negative, to take into account. We all know forty year olds who are unfortunately, but usually by their own efforts, deep into old age. But we also know seventy year olds who think and move like people half their age. They choose to revel in life, to live with passion and so discover a perpetual fountain of youth.

Age is not determinate.. At forty-five George Foreman regained the Heavyweight Boxing Championship of the world. At sixty-eight Colonel Sanders started a fast food empire that spans the globe. At seventy Ronald Reagan became President of the United States. At eighty three Johnny Kelly finished the Boston marathon. But we also know many people who psychologically finished living before age thirty-five. They copped out early. Age is not a predictor of success. It is indeed neutral. Yet age is an extremely common rationalization and excuse that people use to avoid challenge and responsibility. It is only a camouflage.

If you are in your forties for example, and you want to embark on a new career, how would you give yourself the boost you need? You should stop projecting any negative self images and avoid rationalizations into the future. These may fly fast and furious, for there are a thousand reasons that you could list to excuse yourself from pursuing your dream with passion and commitment. But those reasons are really a thousand secret projections. The truth is that no one actually knows what would happen if you devoted your full attention to pursuing your deepest desires.. You could become an apparent failure, which might even be your prediction already. But you might also become a raving success. Who knows? Not even you. So which scenario will you hold on to? What result will you project for all your actions? Success or failure? The answers will determine whether you will have results or excuses in the end.

"I don't know where to begin."

This excuse is surprisingly common in people who have a big dream. Sometimes you just can't get started. There is no one place that you can identify as a good place to take action. You think about it and you talk about it. Then you think about it some more, and you talk about it some more. The wheels keep spinning around ... in your head. The faster they spin, the more elaborate and complicated the plans become. But they produce only plans. There is no ground breaking, no construction and no ribbon to cut.

The antidote for this excuse is probably an irresistible impulse, a moment of inspiration or constraint. You simply 'JUST DO IT'!

One of the most inspiring and exemplary stories of the slogan that Nike made famous is worth repeating here. When the same Mother Theresa received a call to minister to the poorest of the poor in 1947, she promptly left her teaching job in the convent and went to India. She stayed at the home of a friend and just started walking through the streets of Calcutta by herself, ministering to the poor. She met a lot of opposition. She was told that the problems in Calcutta were so severe that her little charity would make no difference at all in the situation. Her response was classic. While cradling a dying man in her arms, she serenely said:

"It makes a difference for *this* man."

And *that* perspective is the key to making a start. If you can't do everything, that is no justification for doing nothing. If you can't embrace it all, you still should not neglect your call. You don't need to have the whole plan. You don't have to know every step. You don't require knowledge of every possible contingency. What you do need is to take action, even if it is the tiniest action imaginable that sets you along the right path. The paralysis that comes to the person who excuses himself with "I don't know where to begin" often derives from trying to find answers to questions that are unanswerable, or trying to find perfection in the imperfect.

There is an old adage: "It is more difficult *thinking* about hard work than actually *doing* it." How true that is. Beginning requires faith ... faith that the answers will come. You need faith to anticipate that the resources will be found and that problems will work themselves out. You must have faith that you will have the stamina and skill you need when you need it, and sometimes not a moment before. Therefore, take a plunge, and have faith. Make a beginning ... and let the consequences unfold as they may.

"I am just too busy."

Many productive individuals focus on time management. They attend practical seminars and gather lots of ideas and the necessary tools to implement a careful and detailed lifestyle habit of managing their time, the only true limited resource. They establish priorities, they use a daily planner and diary, complete with to-do lists and follow-up reminders. Some use hard copy attaché folders, while others exploit the technology of notebook computers and the like. But whatever methodology or scheme you choose, in the final analysis, time cannot truly be managed since it is relatively constant and independent. The challenge comes down to life-management. You must take control of your life to gain some optimization of your use of time.

Capable individuals are usually filling their days with useful activity. They seldom find themselves idle or bored. Yet they are constantly in demand. The best producers are guided by a vision and mission that permit them to make the tough choices and to give their time, effort and energy to the activities they choose. Time, or lack of time, is usually not their problem. They approve of the choices they make and give their best in pursuit of excellence at the tasks they have chosen. They learn to cooperate and to harness the valuable contributions of others through teamwork in any process of execution. They multiply their efforts.

Lack of time is a poor excuse for those who use the lame *'I'm too busy'* to justify *either* the dereliction of valid duty and responsibility, especially in the face of great opportunity, *or* the rationalization of the workaholic treadmill that knows no break or relaxation. For such cowards on the one hand or blind-folded slaves on the other, their excuse is ironic if not paradoxical. The truth of their rationalization is in the adverb '*too*'. They are unbalanced. Their life is out of control, from either the tyranny of lesser duty or the bondage of incessant performance. It is time to wake up - the former to smell 'the coffee', the latter to smell 'the roses'. The former must re-prioritize different assignments and responsibilities, while the latter must re-balance work with leisure and health.

When was the last time you claimed that you were too busy? Did you assess the importance of what you were being called or challenged to do, relative to the present focus and chosen direction of your lifestyle? Did you take the time for reflection? Did you weigh options and alternatives? Could something less be re-assigned? Perhaps more importantly, do you need a break? When was the last time you took a vacation? Have you made a relaxing change lately?

The course of life is a cycle. First, you must work hard, then you should play hard, and then rest well. After resting, then you can resume work again. Where are you in that cycle right now? That should tell you what to do next.

Look at this another way. Responsibility in life is like a pie. Each duty is a slice that combines with the other pieces to make the whole pie, all three hundred and sixty degrees. Much of the time, you will get to cut the pie into pieces of very different sizes. You must constantly assess how you slice your one life to make it taste good to the very last bite. And be careful how and whom you serve.

You are never too *busy*, you can only be *too* busy. Think about that.

"I don't have the money."

Though lack of adequate time may be the excuse of the nineties, lack of money has been the excuse of the ages. Ever since the world of barter, trade and commerce became sophisticated through the use of a common legal tender, it has divided people into two groups, the haves and the have-nots. The have-nots generally assume that those who have can buy-in to anything they choose, while those who have-not are prohibited by their lack of means from doing most of what they would dream or imagine.

In fact, one could divide society into two classes of thinkers. The first group would live by the following premise: "I have $100, so let me see what I can spend it on." They then tailor their activity and even their imagination to the limited use of their $100. The second group in contrast, begins with the question: "What activities would I choose to engage in or what can I imagine for myself?" Having identified their passions and the scope of their vision, they then evaluate their need for income or expenditure cost. Then they go about seeking ways to generate that sum or means in as many creative ways as they can conceive. In the end, the difference in the performance or results of these two groups of people is as different as night and day.

This is a phenomenon where there is no ambiguity between the chicken and the egg. If you begin with a means assessment, then the end is limited by that determined means. There is no growth, no room for expansion, no generation of capital or profit. Whereas if you begin with management by objectives, the human spirit and ingenuity are harnessed to produce the necessary innovation. Ideas are born, solutions are found, growth is stimulated, and there is consequently creation of new wealth. In a word, one must identify goals consistent with one's true passion to trigger the engines of imagination, application and productivity.

Just think about it. You refuse to limit your life by the scope of your present knowledge. You work on your *head-space,* so you think, you learn, you communicate. Similarly, you would not limit your life by the turbulence of your emotions. You work on your *heart-space,* so you seek to be master of all your emotions, to be resilient, to keep a sense of humor and to socialize. You would not even limit your life by the capacity of your skills. You work on your *hand-space* to acquire new techniques and methods, you do research and you capitalize on the expertise of others.

Why then would you limit your life by the depth of your pockets? You must work on your *pocket-space* to find new sources of income or capital; to identify alternative forms of legal tender where you trade in ideas, emotions or technique for investment purposes; and finally, to tap into the vast resource of human potential through leadership. Eventually other people will cooperate and contribute to the realization of the goals you choose for yourself. This is a powerful prescription, worthy of study. Take the time to ponder it carefully.

So what do you really want to do? Does your problem really amount to lack of money? I doubt it. Could that be just a convenient excuse because it is obviously apparent but it truly masks something much more fundamental? Do you have a clear vision? Does it resonate with your passion? Have you engaged your imagination?

Today you can 'multiply your value a hundredfold'. You can take initiatives that will find surprising means in unexpected places. Open your eyes to see the 'cattle on a thousand hills'. Open your mind to receive the one invaluable idea to change your circumstance for the better. Open your heart to let your passion flow and your love reach out to the world. And open your spirit to the One who 'holdeth the wealth of the world in His hands'.

"It's not worth it."

Here is the ultimate excuse of copping out. It is the attempt to silence the constraint of conscience. In the face of opportunity or challenge the first instinctive response is to do justice to your spontaneous desire to have, to do or to be something more. You sense "a bird on the shoulder whispering in the ear 'you should'." But if you are given to making excuses you try to convince yourself that the value of the projected return could not justify the cost or sacrifice required. You downplay the best case scenario of success so that it would lose all appeal and leave you content and at peace with the status quo.

This is much more common than it may appear at first. Clearly, eastern philosophies have favored a false sense of spirituality by suggesting that basic human desire is the antithesis of true maturity and cosmic awareness. They suggest that to approach *Nirvana* is to deny oneself ultimately. It is to lose all sense of strife and struggle. You are encouraged to suppress the urge for material gain or sensual gratification. It is to become at-one with some eternal spirit and consciousness that *is* and is sufficient, with neither need nor want, but only presence and being. Therein is peace, harmony and the tranquillity of the one great soul that captures your being and absorbs your personality into the eternal cycle of truth, love and beauty. You therefore want nothing, need nothing or seek nothing but to be emptied of self, dissolving as it were into the ocean of self-sufficient consciousness.

Such fanciful ideas may appeal to those disillusioned by materialism and consumerism. They may even resonate with the deeper values of clerics, cynics and psychics. But they do no justice to the masses who are destined to suffer from the social, economic and political implications, wherever such philosophies are practiced. They fall short.

Western culture has been dominated by the Judeao-Christian philosophy with its focus on individual responsibility and accountability. As stewards of divine grace and gift, you are called to invest all the resources at your disposal and to use every opportunity to join the Creator in daily acts of service and growth. It is not by coincidence that modern science and technology, as well as stable democracies and public institutions, found their origins in the West. These achievements and all the benefits derived from them, are testimonies to the preeminence of the individual human spirit. They derive from original thought, inflamed by passionate desire to have, to do and to be the best that one can possibly be.

Do you ever question the validity of the opportunity that confronts you? Is this one of your practical excuses for nonchalance or inactivity? The only time this makes reasonable sense is when the particular opportunity is superseded by some *more worthy* challenge. In this response then, you go from the lesser to the greater opportunity, rather than from the small to none at all. Every opportunity has some intrinsic worth, so the answer to the question "is it worth it?" is always "yes". You ought to change the question and not the answer. The better question would be: "Is it worth more than what I am already committed to?" That is the question to assess any desirable change or to prompt some responsible initiative. Anything less is nothing but a vain excuse.

Excuses, excuses, excuses. But if you are prone to make them, you simply cannot get away that easily. Especially if it's all an alibi for ***procrastination***. Waste no more time. Face that reality in the next phase coming up ...now!

* * *

The Evolution of **YES!** *unfolds:*

You must risk participation

as you pursue your dream

without excuse!

7

Procrastination

("One of these days")

I almost put-off writing this section of the book. No, not really. But I was tempted to, or more precisely, the thought did go through my mind, just as it would yours. As we actively pursue the life of positive affirmation, of expressed passion and high productivity, surely we cannot escape this tendency to procrastinate. We tend to *put off* everything.

PUT OFF ...

The scenario is so common that it almost qualifies as a folk myth, even though we watch it happen to countless men and women every single day. That's a reference to people who have put their lives on hold. In the back of their minds they think that *"one of these days"* they will take the plunge into a passionate and fulfilled life. They have active minds.

They have planned their plans and dreamed their dreams, and they can tell you exactly, often in astonishing detail, what they are going to do to fulfill their deepest longing ... *one of these days*. Not today, you understand, because today is full of obligations and responsibilities. Today is already overflowing with the busyness of meeting their daily commitments. But *one of these days* ... "look out, you'll see".

Oh what a sad thing it is to witness those dreams put on hold, to watch lives slip into neutral gear, grasping at the promise of some other elusive time. Do those days ever arrive? Do those folks ever climb the ladder of urgent applications and dive off the high board into the excitement and pleasure of a life committed to making precious dreams come alive today? Some eventually do, but for all too many people "*one of these days*" never really comes.

So much of life has the taste of aching regret. When someone passes on from this life, we sometimes think of what else could and should have been made out of such a promising life. We rail against fate but often fate has little to do with it. The real malady is so much less romantic. In fact, the problem is quite pedestrian. When we deny our compelling dreams or suspend our deepest passions, and when we defer the collective longings of our secret desires, we are putting our very lives on hold. It is a dangerous affliction, yet it has at its source nothing more glamorous than the simple human tendency to procrastinate.

This bad habit that often seems so innocuous and is so

widespread, this behavior that is so very human, is in reality like a hundred pound deadweight that presses us down and squeezes the lifeblood from us. Ironically, we put off the joys and responsibilities of life, only to inherit a burden that haunts our steps and eventually stops us dead in our tracks. Sometimes literally so, we *slip off* the high road.

SLIP OFF ...

Is there any human foible more universal than procrastination? We certainly start young. The very moment that you are aware of having responsibility for something, be it making up your bed, tidying up your room, mowing the grass or handing in homework, procrastination steals into your consciousness, initiating a lifelong battle that you must struggle with on a daily basis.

Procrastination wears a mask of soft innocence. It usually seems so harmless and almost reverent. The library book on your car seat is now four weeks overdue. The dental appointment will be made soon, of course. The car will get its tune-up sometime before it refuses to start. You leave the stack of letters unmailed on your desk for a week. You put off calling your sick aunt. You leave the expense report in your briefcase until no more cash advances are allowed. You avoid unclogging the drain in the basement until you can almost canoe from the washing machine to the furnace. All the while you are confident that in the end, everything will work out just fine. That's the way it is. Or is it?

One of the great outlets for procrastination today is the Internet. Many thousands of computer owners and operators have great intentions of getting on the Net. They talk about it, read about it and even make plans for what they can do to exploit it. But they are still off it. They will eventually get on "the road to the future", *one of these days.* They may be losing business, missing opportunities, neglecting ideas and information that could have major impact on their personal world. But they will get to that ... later. *One of these days.*

Ironically, the Internet even brings us a game called Procrastination. And if you search for it there, you will even find *a humorous version* of ***The Procrastinator's Creed*** which looks something like this (the brackets are mine):

1. *I believe that if anything is worth doing, it has already been done.*   (So why bother?)

2. *I will never put off until tomorrow, what I can forget about forever.* (There's the ultimate solution for stress management.)

3. *I know the work cycle isn't plan/start/finish, it is really wait/wait/plan.* (Then wait some more.)

4. *I shall always start, begin, initiate, take the first step whenever I get around to it.* (Then make yourself a round TUIT like Zig Ziglar did.)

5. *I will never rush into a project without weighing the consequences, right down to the last pictogram.* (You'll never be a Heavyweight.)

6. *I firmly believe that the future holds breathtaking discoveries, technological miracles, and fresh innovations that will relieve me from my obligations.* (Your heart and brain will still remain.)

7. *I follow the Great Law of Reciprocal Importance--the more important the task that needs to be completed, the more insignificant the work is that needs to be finished first.* (It's all relative.)

8. *I shall never forget that the probability of a miracle occurring, although microscopically small, is still not absolute zero.* (It must take a miracle not to believe in miracles.)

9. *I shall hold fast to the real truth--early birds feel wretched all day.* (The late birds have no feeling at all.)

10. *I am truly convinced that for all the talk of deadlines, no one has ever died from missing them.* (They died from not having them.)

You get the idea. Procrastination becomes a harmless diversion that we can gently mock. I am all for the lighter side of life, and looking at our troubles with humor and humility, but procrastination is not quite as harmless as one may suppose.

From my perspective as a physician, I see procrastination of many little things as symptoms of a bigger and more dangerous disease. As we might say medically, there is a real pathology here. Although there may be no harm in putting off the small things in life, never fail to realize the slow and steady progression--and the inevitable consequences--of the procrastinator's approach. It is a slippery slope indeed.

How many people have put off that doctor's visit, only to find later, on examination, serious consequences that could possibly have been avoided? Think of the person who runs out of gasoline on the interstate highway, miles from any station, having passed regular service centers but put off filling up until the next exit. Think of the businessman who wants to cut costs or sell a losing enterprise, but he delays action until declaring bankruptcy becomes the only option.

What examples have you known where simple procrastination such as "*one of these days*" has led to serious consequences? Are you in danger of sliding down a slope of procrastination that ends in really muddy waters? It is time to *face-off* with this enemy of success.

FACE OFF ...

The first step on the road to overcoming procrastination so that you can really say **YES!** to life, is to start seeing procrastination for the life-wrecker that it very often becomes. If you want to overcome procrastination, you have to first start taking it seriously. And you can't put off doing just that. If you have a real tendency to procrastinate, there is one little tool I came across that can be very helpful. It is something I picked up for the computer.

This particular software package first records your birthday and your gender. It then calculates your typical life expectancy using actuarial averages. Finally, it posts a big notice on your computer screen every day when you turn the machine on. The notice is a large number that tells you how many days you could, would or should (depending!) have left to live your life. What a fabulous splash of cold water every single day! The real element of genius or folly (depending!) in this program, is that it gives you a daily reminder of two absolutely crucial facts. Fact One: your life is finite, it has an ending. It has so many days (depending!) and then no more. Fact Two: your life is getting shorter each and every day. Every day you are running out of time.

Without doubt, it is a sobering moment each day when the computer goes on and the number is reduced by one digit. And it is true, many people might complain that it is too morbid or moving a routine (depending!). Who wants to be reminded on a daily basis of the inevitability of death? Well, I can think of several unfortunate patients, friends, colleagues ... who probably would not have objected, in retrospect. They gambled on the future and they lost.

To overcome procrastination, first and foremost you have to recognize and even affirm that procrastination matters. It is important and must be dealt with, for the tendency will never go away spontaneously. The worst procrastinators sleepwalk through life with a vague hope that things will get better. They insist that tomorrow holds promises that are unrealized today. They believe that waiting is the answer to every question and the strategy for every problem. How wonderful it would be for them to get a moment of clarity, to really see the heartbreaking path they have set themselves on. How much better it would be for them to lay hold of life now with every ounce of urgency, passion, excitement and energy that they possess.

May I gently suggest that if you would pursue a life of **YES!** with all the joy and gusto that that implies, then do not toy with the mirth of procrastination because there is nothing funny about it. Throw away that previous Procrastinator's Creed and embrace the moment. Seize the present with both hands, with head and with heart. Wrap this sacred bundle called **NOW** with tenderness and care, then guard it jealously as if your life depended on it, for it does.

On this earth as we know it, there is no life but in the now. That is a healthy and pragmatic existentialism. The truth is that life is only the continuum or string of connected moments. Our passion and purpose give both dimension and direction to that string of time, over time.

Here are some affirmative suggestions for living and acting in the present moment.

A New Creed for the Procrastinator:

1. *I will give thanks every morning for another day, with the full knowledge that there are some people who did not wake up.*

2. *I will promise myself to seize each and every day and live it as if it were my last.*

3. *I will remember that Opportunity knocks most often on the doors that are opened quickest.*

4. *If anything is worth doing then I will do it A.S.A.P. (as soon as possible)*

5. *I will reject a life with no risks as a very poor euphemism for a life with no rewards.*

6. *I will prove to myself that action is the taproot of a passionately lived life.*

7. *I will not put off for tomorrow what can be done today, for tomorrow never comes.*

8. *Since I value my relationships, I will treat them like gold today.*

9.   *I will promise myself that at the end of my life I will have results, not excuses.*

10.   *I will write my own epitaph: "He/She made the absolute most out of the talents, gifts and opportunities that they were given; they gave life everything they had and then some. They were afraid of running out of time."*

Until you start to treat procrastination seriously, you will never be able to mount the kind of psychological, physical and spiritual assault you need to overcome this debilitating personality flaw. It is even more than a flaw, it is like a disease of the soul.

Do you remember the Parable of the Ten Virgins? Five were wise and five were foolish. The former secured adequate oil supplies *early* while the others delayed. When the bridegroom came, the wise virgins went in to meet Him and the door was shut. By the time the procrastinators returned after fetching what they could, it was too late. They ran out of time. That's serious. It's fatal. A word to the *wise* is usually sufficient.

Procrastination is a soul disease that causes great harm. First, here and now, and later, there and then. Over time it becomes a way of life. We described it as a core personality flaw, but then it becomes like a malignant disease that can overrun your entire life.

The result of procrastination is that you begin to live

life in suspended pause. Your daily experience becomes full of responsibilities that hold no allure to your deepest passions. Life is deferred. You are putting in time, just passing the hours, no more and no less. But your very life is then on hold. Instead, you need to rise up and *fight-off* the curse.

FIGHT OFF ...

There are many helpful strategies in overcoming procrastination. But none of them will be successful unless you adopt an attitude that nurtures them. Human beings are born with a basic instinctive hormonal reaction to danger that is called the 'fight or flight' response. You either flee from danger, or you prepare yourself to fight. It is a *subconscious* reflex response.

The same response, although neither hormonal nor instinctive, operates at the conscious level as well. When you have a burdensome but important chore to carry out that is either boring, unpleasant or tedious, you can have two possible reactions. Reaction One: you can flee, run away, avoid the task.   That is obviously the response of procrastination. Then there is Reaction Two: you can fight, you can dig in, you can grit your teeth and soldier forward. You can refuse to give in to procrastination by *conscious* choice. This is not a reflex but it can become a conditioned response. (More about that later.) At least, you can do something.

The ultimate fantasy of a procrastinating mind is to hope that if you do nothing, your bad habit of procrastination will eventually disappear. But if your dreams are precious to you, you must fight for them. If your goals resonate with your true self, then contend for them. If you choose a life of excitement and accomplishment, then press forward now. Fight for it. Fight! Wrestle the enemy of procrastination to the ground. Withstand the crafty suggestion to defer to some later time whatever drives your passion now. **NOW!**

There is an old adage in therapy circles that says 'there is no way *around* our problems and the only way out is *through* the problem.' The same holds true for the people who have fallen victim to procrastination. Many a person invests hundreds of hours in therapy trying to discover a pain-free way to shed bad habits. But you can forget about the shortcuts. Anyone with a serious case of procrastination will never really get rid of it until they get accustomed to doing things they don't *want* to do. Many of the things you procrastinate about, really are unpleasant. So why spend time and money trying to figure out why these things are unpleasant and why you shun them? Wouldn't you be better off just accepting these unpleasant realities and taking action?

Success in any field requires that you spend a great deal of time doing things that you may very well hate. Smart people get accustomed to that and accept it. Procrastinators rationalize, excuse and justify why they don't do what really needs to be done, while constantly spinning their wheels. Procrastination is something you have to fight your way through. But the payoff can be a life lived with excitement, reward and accomplishment. Therefore the struggle is a small price to pay. So *jump off* the edge of your comfort zone.

JUMP OFF ...

Procrastinators wait and wait and wait. They wait for a better time, the right time, the perfect time. Today is still not the tomorrow that they talked about yesterday. They intend to, they plan to, they hope to. Their desire seems as good as action. In any case, they will do it soon. But soon becomes sometime, sometime becomes anytime, anytime becomes no time--never. The truth is that the remedy of the disease, the answer to the problem is to ... JUMP OFF!

Here's how.

1.   ***Talk to yourself.*** This is a great habit to get into. Whenever procrastination gets to be a problem, use the "two column" technique. Get a blank piece of paper. Start by writing all of your excuses for procrastinating on the left hand side of the paper,

giving yourself plenty of space between excuses. On the right hand side of the page, you can counter the excuses, one by one, with realistic thoughts that defeat each alibi disguised as argument.

2.   *Use affirmations.* Keep a growing list of positive statements that you can use to stimulate action when procrastination starts to become a problem. For example,

> *"Life is lived in the moment, in the eternal now, which is the source of the only human freedom I have."*
>
> *"The longer I wait, the worse the procrastination gets. I will do it now when it is cheaper and less painful."*
>
> *"Perfectionism doesn't exist in human endeavor. It is an illusion that keeps me from acting in the present moment."*
>
> *"The sooner I finish it, the more fun and the more peace of mind I will have later."*
>
> *"Doing the work is a lot less agonizing than thinking about doing the work."*

Make a hobby of collecting quotes from people you admire most and create a category for overcoming procrastination.

3. ***Avoid mental catastrophes.*** If you fear the task at hand, you will put it off. Jumping to the conclusion that you are no good at something or that you are going to fail will only create a wall of fear that will stop you cold. If you think you'll fail, you've lost. If you think you can't, you won't. Negative predictions are not facts. They are self-fulfilling prophecies. You must avoid them. Focus on the present and on what positive steps you can take toward reaching your goals in the future.

4. ***Design your goals.*** Think about what you want and what needs to be done. Be specific. Figure out a mini timeline with realistic goals at each step. Write them down. Keep your sights within reason. Having goals that are too big can defeat you right from the start. Don't be surprised by your new fountain of energy and ideas. That's what goals generate.

5. ***Set priorities.*** Ironically, a daily to-do list is a procrastinator's best friend. You must first write down all that needs to be done today. Then arrange the list in order of importance. The greater the urgency, the greater the priority. Then start at the top and work your way down the list. What a simple idea but what a possible dramatic effect on efficiency and productivity. Watch your stress level fall.

6. ***Break any project into smaller tasks***. Big projects tend to overwhelm us. Break them into small and manageable parts. You'll get more done if you do it piece by piece. Make sure that unpleasant tasks especially are in small parts. We can usually do something unpleasant if we know that it is only for a little while. Remember 'Life by the yard, is hard; life by the inch, is a cinch'.

7. ***Take a stand.*** Are you familiar with what are called *Ebenezer Stones*? They are markers of progress. Like stakes in the ground, they make land claims. They identify the territory you've covered. They post your presence. Now take a stand, make a commitment, a promise that you will live by. Write yourself a contract that you can sign. Better yet, tell a friend, a spouse or family member about your commitment. Most importantly, marking Ebenezer Stones can help you acknowledge that you are not alone, that you have help and so you can live by faith.

8. ***Use prompts***. Write reminders to yourself of the tasks you have to do and the goals you have to pursue. Put them in conspicuous places, like the bathroom mirror, the refrigerator and the car dashboard. The more your plans are actively on your

mind, the greater the likelihood that you will carry them out.

9. ***Reward yourself.*** Self re-enforcement has a powerful effect on developing a "do it now" attitude. Celebrate often. Pat yourself on the back and let yourself enjoy even the smallest accomplishments. So, take your spouse to dinner. Buy some new shoes or your favorite fragrance. Enjoy each victory and savor its taste, however you choose.

10. ***Act now***. Don't put off implementing these very practical suggestions. Stop reading this book for a short while. Review Make some clear **decisions**. Can you? Take definitive action. Do it now. Now!

* * *

The Evolution of **YES!** *unfolds:*

You must risk participation

as you pursue your dream,

without excuse

now!

● — ● — ● — ● — ● — ● — ● — ○ — ○ — ○ — ○ — ○

8

Indecision

("Perhaps")

A wise philosopher once concluded that we are the sum total of all the decisions we have made throughout our lives. In a very real way, life is an unfolding journey and the path we take on that journey is one that we very much *choose* for ourselves. Along that path there are many forks in the road and each one represents a decision. Day after day we are constantly having to make those choices, big and small, by the hundreds if not thousands. We choose where to live, the kind of work we do, the spouse we live with, how many children if any, the clothes we wear, to smoke or not to smoke, the investments we make, the friends we associate with, whether to have dessert, how much exercise we do, what to do on vacation, and on and on.

These are choices. Some are more obvious than others, especially if the decisions are easy or spontaneous. In some situations there is a gut-wrenching loneliness when you have to make major change. But it is only through that tunnel of decision that you must enter in order to reap the rewards of freedom and the joy of affirmative living. Your ability to be decisive will play a large role in determining the course of your life and obviously how much success, joy and fulfillment you will get out of life.

Your decisions define your agenda. You must *choose* to define your own agenda or someone else will define their agenda and choose for you. How true that is of so many, and oh how sad it is!

ANGST

Slowly we are becoming a nation of fence-sitters. We act often like tentative mice who hang back and wait, indecisive and unclear about the direction we should take. This can derive along the path we have seen thus far, from a poor self image and vicarious existence, or from a lack of internal constraint and values, lack of focus, fear of risk, or a tendency to make excuses and to procrastinate. But even if you surmount all those hurdles as you progress along this evolutionary course to positive, passionate and productive living, you can still be handicapped by indecision.

Indecision is a pernicious malady, a disease that slowly eats away at your integrity. If your goal is to develop a style of living that exclaims **YES!** to life, then this corrosive element of indecisiveness is clearly another candidate for the housekeeping that we have been doing, as we continue to trace the evolutionary path to **YES!**

Saying **YES!** to life is itself a decision and it provides you with just one more reason why you have to learn the skillful art of taking the plunge, of throwing yourself into your journey without reservation, of putting your heart and soul into the work you have undertaken. While fence-sitters never find themselves on the wrong side of the fence, they also never get a chance to run in the meadow. They do not smell the sweet lilacs that bloom in springtime, or dangle their feet in the mountain stream. They are in a real sense forfeiting the fruits of joyful living, while they try to protect themselves from the   potential consequences of a wrong decision.

Where do we see this trait of indecision manifested in the lives of the people around us? Everywhere.

It could be an engaged couple who have dated for years and stand at the threshold of marriage, clearly unable to make up their minds to take the final step. They are oblivious to the fact that they are investing the precious currency of their young lives in nervous indecision and getting a poor return. Modern common-law relationships are sometimes arrangements of convenience or else deliberate protests of social dissidents who choose to confront the status quo. At other times though, it is the path of least resistance, reflecting the lack of real commitment by the couple. It is leaving a door of reservation open, as if their decision to stick together is equivocal or uncertain and therefore unpredictable. The decline of the modern family with more than fifty percent of marriages ending prematurely in divorce, reflects in part the social malaise of indecision and compromise.

Indecision could likewise be seen in the young corporate executive or manager whose career path has squeezed them into a straight jacket, where the politics of power dominate over the influence of ideas and skills. Work is no longer exciting or personally challenging. But they may have what it would take to find a colorful parachute and make a successful jump. If only they would leave the corporate security blanket. They may wrestle for years with the decision to start their own business, patiently waiting for "a time that is right" to decide. It will likely never come. So they endure the corporate crap and they still don't sleep well. They hustle. They make some progress, only to discover that *"whoever wins the rat-race still remains a rat."*

Or consider the indecisive single man who stands gazing at the beautiful countenance of a woman he has admired from a distance for months, patiently rehearsing the lines he would use if they should ever meet. But he never manages to summon the courage to actually approach or engage her in conversation. He can't decide to *enter* into a relationship. That's one extreme. Then contrast the indecisive victims of abuse who can't decide to leave their alcoholic husbands and fathers. They feel trapped by their own rationalization and dependence. For years they can endure the pain, the shame, the exploitation, the humiliation. But at each encounter, when the time comes to act, to pack up and leave or to report the villains and lock the door, they fall back in empathy or fear, in weakness or dependency. It's a circular cage. In the final analysis, they wrestle with indecision and lose, again and again. They can't decide to *end* the relationship. Just another example of the failure to be affirmative and to say **YES!** to themselves and to *their* future.

We can add many more illustrative examples very easily because the ranks of the indecisive are broad and deep. But before we take a look at some of the elements that lead to habitual indecision, let's first take a look at its real cost. What is the price to be paid for the fence-sitting that is so endemic in our society?

COST

Those who cling to the emotional comfort of indecision pay a very high price for the "privilege." What feels like prudence in vacillating, waiting and drifting, turns out to be nothing more than a rut. It defines a place so narrow, confining and limited that if we are not careful, one could spend months and years stuck there, slowly pacing back and forth, putting in the miles but going nowhere. Random walk processes (to use a scientific term) produce a net displacement which is always a very small fraction of the total distance covered by the walk. It's akin to going around in irregular and incomplete circles. You may beat the air, but in reality, go nowhere. Or think of swimming against a strong current, making hundreds of strokes but gaining little ground in the water.

Without the mental resolve to clearly make a decision and the commitment that goes with it, many people end up living life on "automatic pilot". They go from one place to another, from one poor habit to the next. They move from job to job, and relationship to relationship, as the prevailing current carries them. You could call their lifestyle "unconscious living". Socrates called it the "unexamined life". The net result is the same.

These people can agonize over the path they feel called to follow to such an extent that their knotted stomachs even tie up their feet, and so their progress is greatly diminished. For such people their life is like that of an empty bottle adrift at sea, bouncing in the waves. They are first carried in one direction and then another, completely subject to the wind and waves, traveling wherever the elements carry it. No doubt many miles are covered that way and the journey includes new sights and sounds, and even some novelties. But whether they will enjoy the journey or reach a desirable destination is another matter, because nothing that happens is of their own choosing. They have no true life of their own springing from the inside out.

As you live your life, you are all subject to inertia; you develop momentum pointed in the direction you are traveling. Once your direction and momentum stabilize, if you do not decide to take control, you will pretty much stay on an assumed track for your entire life. This is true of the career you settle in, the standard of living you accept, the social cliques you bond with, the religious and cultural values you adopt, the lifestyle habits you engage, et cetera.

Those of us from a scientific background would be very familiar with Sir Isaac Newton's First Law of Dynamics: *any **object** continues in a state of rest or uniform motion in a straight line unless outside forces act upon it.* That was used to describe the inanimate world of physics. It was devoid of will, of desire, of brain power, of character, of all that makes us human.

But that law of Newton can easily be used to describe the way many of us lead our own lives. It is as if, in effect, we lose the essence of our humanity, i.e. a mind of our own, a passionate heart and a will to chose our own destiny. Once we get set on a path, it seems extra difficult and sometimes highly impossible to change our course, without introducing some massive *outside* force to act as an agent of change.

Yet that change need not come from the outside. It can come from the inside. We are not objects. We are living human beings and laws of biology often run diametrically opposed to laws of inanimate physics. Introduce qualities of the soul - mind, heart and will - and this changes everything.

Is there a science of love? Is determinism in our genes? Is the imagination confined to neurons? Let us celebrate the essence of being human.

Indecision threatens to destroy the essence of what makes us human. By choosing, you affirm what you are, and who you are, and so elect to live your individual life. If you fail to decide the course of life that you will follow, you frustrate and negate your human will. You stifle and obliterate your human mind and then you suppress and siphon your human passion, the very heart and soul of life itself. That is an awfully high price to pay.

Change, simply put, can rest in your willingness to take a stand, to be decisive. You can make a decision and then make that decision yours to live by. Clear and bold decisions are invigorating; they focus and energize us in a way that nothing else will. The clearest and simplest way to get off automatic pilot is through the awesome power of a decision. You can just decide.

Oh what a liberating and stimulating experience awaits anyone who can make a decision and then make it theirs! So stop equivocating and take the plunge. That is the natural and legitimate expression of who you are.

OPPORTUNITY

It is quite common to hear people complain about the lack of opportunity. They claim that they want to improve their situation and to get more out of life. But they have never had a chance. They are waiting for their big break. Somehow, somewhere they expect a door to fly open.

In Phase Five of *The Evolution of YES!* we observed how many people have resigned themselves to the idea that the only opportunities they have in life derive from the almost infinitesimal chance of winning something, and usually the bigger, the better. On the whole, most people often see real big opportunity as a scarce and select resource that is bestowed only on the rich, the talented or gifted individuals, and of course, on the lucky folks. But never on themselves.

Nothing could be further from the truth. Opportunity surrounds you. It beckons you. Opportunity is yours for the asking, or perhaps better said, yours for the *deciding*. And you wonder what is this perpetual fountain of opportunity? And how do you tap into it?

At its most fundamental level, you and I all enjoy opportunity each and every day when we awake and face a brand new day. Providence has been kind to us, separating our lives into individual twenty-four hour cycles. This makes every morning very much like a daily rebirth. Who else but God could have ingeniously designed such a wise and loving gift? It is as if we were dispensed all the bounty of nature one mouthful at a time so we could chew it, digest it, absorb it and use the inherent value to our ultimate good. We can live each day, squeezing its richness to prove that its joy is good to the last drop.

So you can arise each morning and decide something new. You can decide to put your fears behind you and take a stand for what you believe in. You can decide to shake off the lethargy and get excited again about your dreams. You can decide that life is still a simple proposition... *you get out of life what you put into it...* and choose to put in more. You can decide to have what you really want, to do whatever you have real passion to accomplish, and to become the best that you can possibly be.

But to take advantage of today's opportunity, you need the ability to make a clear choice. You must be decisive, and grasp what you really want. All the power of daily living flows from the power of resolute decision, of choosing a specific personal goal and then committing to it. You can harness the streams that flow daily into your life and focus all of them to serve the realization of that goal. When that energy is focused, it will ignite, it will cause something to happen and the opportunity will explode. But when you are caught in the trap of indecisiveness, you cut yourself off from the opportunities that continually present themselves to you. Indecision and lost opportunity always walk hand in hand. Decisiveness is the key to embracing your opportunity.

By now you are getting the idea of how central this ability to make a clear decision is. It not only opens the door to opportunity but it also is a springboard to personal growth. Let me explain.

There are many perspectives we can adopt in trying to understand the meaning of life.   One of the perspectives that makes the most sense and sheds the most light on the struggle of life, is that you and I are here on this planet to grow, to become what we were meant to be.   And in part, this struggle involves solving problems, transcending difficult circumstances and clarifying values.   To do all that you need to make choices.   You will never have the opportunity to grow or to become the person that you were meant to be, if you hang back tentatively refusing to commit yourself to anything.   Without the power of decisiveness you have no impetus to make the difficult choices that serve as the foundation stones for personal growth.   Life begins to stagnate behind a web of cautious reticence.

When you choose, it is as if you exercise some spiritual muscle.   With repeated use, those muscles seem to grow stronger and more resilient.   You grow in character, maturity and strength.   At the same time, you gain confidence and you are encouraged and motivated to take initiative, to reach out and make a difference in the world.   All because you dare to make clear decisions.   It is an indispensable step on the road to an unequivocal **YES!**

If our generation could become as obsessed about mental and spiritual exercise as we have about bodily exercise and fitness, just image what a revolution would come about in the real quality of life.

CLOSURE

But making a clear decision is often easier said than done. Serious decision making is the loneliest activity in the world. After all the advice and input, it comes down to the internal resolution of desires, values, interests and the like. It is sometimes like tearing Velcro inside the stomach. It is pulling away one thing from another when both options are not possible.

Let us not kid ourselves, many decisions are not easy to make. A difficult decision often requires patience and discipline. Before making the decision, the alternatives have to be carefully weighed against the expected consequences. These may not be, and often are not predictable. Hence, the apprehension. Sometimes the final decision can be agonizing. But still the agony ought not to prevent us from actually making a clear and definite choice. We learn to say **YES!** to the clearest and best alternative, as we also choose to say **NO** to another.

The only way to get rid of the old is to make a decision that will put it to rest. That's the urgency of getting down off the fence. It's called closure. It allows you to move on, to get on to the next challenge or task, to pursue new horizons. It takes effort and energy to stay there on the fence with no clear decision. Rest and peace are at ground level, on one side or the other. And when facing a decision, that's what you have to discover. You get off on either side and the choice will at least then be obvious.

There can be no doubt at all that indecision is a big contributor to poor mental hygiene. As you vacillate over decisions, the negative emotions start to build. Feelings of frustration, regret, neurosis and guilt begin to grow. The more time you spend spinning your wheels in making a decision, the more these negative emotions build without a release, sometimes to the point of even being psychologically debilitating.

So good mental hygiene is dependent on your ability to make decisions with conviction, sweeping away the old through closure, while making room for the new. You may have a psychological backlog that needs to be cleared and nothing will clear it out quite as quickly as a newly found resolve to be decisive.

Just think of decisions that you still have to make, even now. In reality, they are blocked arteries in your life waiting for incisive resolution to restore the flow of passion, energy, creativity ... life! Why wait?

There is even more to be gained from making that clear decision. All of us like to be able to look with satisfaction on concrete things that represent the fruits of our labor, the expression of our ideas. There is something about seeing tangible results that gives us pride of accomplishment, something that really forms the foundation stones of self-confidence. We come to believe in our own abilities through a series of achievements that help us build a sense of mastery in our world.

But what chance do you have to build anything lasting or permanent (or eternal, for that matter), if you are paralyzed from ever taking a stand and making a decision, then making it yours, and following through like never before?

Decisiveness and a sense of accomplishment are truly inexorably bound together.

STRUGGLE

And yet I know some of you reading this will still be struggling. Quietly you face the challenge of the future with inner voices beckoning you to make a move, to get involved, to pursue your dream, to reach out, to make a difference ... and I can almost hear you whisper to yourself, *'Perhaps'*. You are still not quite sure. You remain indecisive about what you really want to do, or even what you should do. To say **YES!** means a change of your status quo. Your equilibrium will be disturbed. You will lose some privacy. You'll become vulnerable. You might even fail. Therefore, you wrestle with indecision.

So, why are most people so indecisive?

For some people, a decision is threatening to their freedom. Once it is definitively made, it cuts off other opportunities. For example, a single person in a committed relationship has two choices that are possible. First, they can continue being single, or second, they can get married. But once they are married, their choices will have disappeared. 'That's it. It's over'. So some people see decisions as being limiting, as being an encroachment on their freedom. They want to keep all of their options open as long as possible.

But what is the value of options until at least one of them is exercised? The value of choice only exists if and when that choice is made. There's the paradox of decision making.

An extreme case of this phenomenon is seen when free-spirited people sing the praises of an open mind, conceiving of it as an end, in and of itself. They hold to no absolute views on any subject because they would see that as a contradiction to their apparent virtue of open-mindedness. But they have failed to realize that an open mind is a means and not an end in itself. It is the means by which we filter information without bias, as we continue on our journey towards truth. Yet when an open mind comes upon truth, it ought to embrace that truth like a legtrap. It can only remain open while in search of veritable truth. To remain open after that is to deny being open in the first place. It reminds me of the agnostic I once heard boasting that he was *"absolutely sure that no one could be sure of anything"*. But as the saying goes, I guess 'there is none so blind as the one who would not see'.

The same is true when it comes to indecisiveness. Maintaining freedom of choice is a means and not an end. We like to keep all of our options open so that we do not needlessly become entrenched in something that adds no spark or fire to our imagination. We reject anything that neither has claim on our passion nor resonates with our conviction. Yet that freedom ought to be freely given up when we come across a choice that deserves our time, energy and commitment. We then choose because we are challenged. We decide because we feel the excitement of the opportunity that we envisage and because we find consistency with our values. We can make that clear decision to say **YES!** because some option is both apparent to the mind but more so, it is appealing to the heart.

Sometimes plain old-fashioned greed leads to indecisiveness. We try to conjure up a plan that will allow us to enjoy the fruits of both alternatives. Until we also learn to say NO, no decision is forthcoming. But then, a strong **NO!** to one option can often amount to a defined **YES!** to another. If we are certain of what we don't want, that could dictate exactly what we do. That means letting some things go. Even some good things.

How reassuring it is to recognize that you can enjoy the fullness of life and taste the fruits of your passion without having everything, doing everything, being everywhere or simply always saying **YES!**

Some people are such perfectionists that they find it impossible to make a clear decision. Unless something can be done perfectly, at least to their satisfaction, it will not be done at all. So they bide their time, marshaling the resources that they feel they will need to execute the plan perfectly. They seem to be unaware that perfection is not a human construct and is entirely unworthy to act as the canter of all our goals and objectives.

The perfect decision just does not exist and neither does the perfectly executed plan. Yet many people are stuck in indecisiveness as they work towards these impossible goals. How liberating to recall that you are not called to perfection. You would need omniscience to exercise perfect judgment in decision-making and that is reserved for the Divine who inhabits eternity. You must decide in time, in context, in hope, and then resign to live with the consequences. Welcome to the world of *homo sapiens.*

Others owe their indecisiveness to a fear of failure and a lack of confidence in their abilities. They are never certain whether things will go right or wrong, so they hold back, on the edge, waiting until they have more confidence in their abilities. But ironically, it is the very act of decision-making that builds confidence.

A failure to decide is itself a decision. That is the null solution, which usually means that nothing happens. Time, talent and truth are all wasted. On the road to **YES!** it is equivalent to moving backwards.

THE BIG ONE

Finally therefore, I want you to consider the really big decision ... your big decision.

So where exactly does decisiveness fit into the big picture, when it comes to saying **YES!** to life? In some respects the whole discussion so far has been a prologue, a warm up, a presentation of a psychological difficulty that it is important to overcome. But what is the real concern?

The real concern is not so much that people are indecisive about jobs and houses, or about relationships and careers, although all of those things are important. The real issue is that people are indecisive about the biggest decision of all ... *'Am I going to choose to live my life on my own agenda now, with passion and excitement, or am I going to simply go through the motions dictated by someone else?* Will my activity and behavior derive from what I choose to believe in, and what I give my heart and soul to? Or, will I go through the motions with no heart'? If the heart dies, you will die.   Inside, at first.   In the final analysis, the biggest waste that results from indecisiveness is *the waste of a life.*

So, are *you* going to go after what *you* really want?

Decisiveness is all about being a leader and not just a follower. It is about growing instead of stagnating and slowly dying. When you make a clear decision you choose to let your light shine in the world instead of sitting and cursing the darkness.

Are you focused on a super abundant life of action and meaning, a life of values and relationships that you create and sustain in a dynamic way? Do you want to be on the inside, a keen participant, an intimate acquaintance of people who are doing exciting things with their life? Or are you going to remain satisfied, just standing on the outside looking in, wondering what it is really like inside? The view is so much different on the inside looking out, compared to being on the outside looking in.

Where do you stand? What have you decided? Are you ready to take the plunge? Are you ready to accept total responsibility for your life and to dive in, head or even heart first? Once you make that decision, once you decide that anything less than a passionate drive for the fruits of life is second best, you have made *the* Big Decision and all the rest will spring from that decision like the ripple effect that a stone makes when it is thrown into a lake.

That is what this book is all about. Shake off the cobwebs. Loosen your shoulders. Limber up your legs. Life is a parade and it is a far better thing to be marshall of your parade, than to stand on the sidelines watching other people experience the real joy of their active living. Make your decision count. And even more important, make it yours.

Now, don't be *shy*!

* * *

The Evolution of **YES!** *unfolds:*

You must risk participation
as you pursue your dream,
without excuse now, by making a
clear decision!

9

Shyness

("I really want to")

You have come a long way in *The Evolution of YES!*
You are far removed from the abyss of negativism and defeat,
no longer content to just look on while others enjoy life's
best. You are now constrained from within and rising to the
challenge being offered, without conditions. You know you
would like to live with passion and you even dare to use your
fertile imagination to full advantage. With all excuses
eliminated, you refuse to procrastinate anymore. You
therefore made a clear decision to go for it, to pursue what
you want to have, to do and to be.

But as some come to the threshold of saying **YES!**,
they find that as much as they really want to, they are
inhibited. They feel and act with a reticence unbecoming of
their desire and commitment. They are victims of a common
personality trait. They stand at the door of opportunity or at

the challenging water's edge where they hesitate to enter in, simply because they are shy. A common condition indeed.

In some circles, or at least under certain circumstances, shyness has developed an allure or an appeal over the years. We often equate shyness with the mystery or mystique of hidden treasures and forbidden secrets. And so it should be, because in the realm of romantic relationships, a subtle coyness only serves to multiply the intrigue and desire for the paramour. Potential romantic liaisons are filled with the promise of pleasant surprises and untold delights. There is a certain magic there, a veil of innocence. Shyness can almost be seductive, like a veil covering the personality. So for the sake of discussion in this Phase, let's leave the romantics alone.

That type of romantic shyness is not the problem when you face the obstacles that get in the way of a passionate or a fulfilled life. Not at all. The real problem is much more pedestrian and commonplace. In fact, it is boringly unromantic. The type of shyness that we want to elaborate on is one that spontaneously handicaps many people in the common expressions of daily living. It holds them back from ordinary socializing and making friends, or from pursuing job prospects. It deters them from expressing their simple wishes in the daily bustle of commerce, or from reaching out to take initiative and seize opportunity, or from just exploring many possibilities at hand. It is in these areas that so many struggle and fail. Such shyness can certainly hold one back from the life of **YES!**

As we consider this, it becomes necessary to untangle the underlying threads that produce this type of shyness. It is not surprising that this social disposition is manifest at an early age. Children are unique and temperamentally different. They are molded by their environment, yes, but they do begin to shape their own *persona* early. They later make assertive choices in adolescence to reflect their own self-image. And the consequences are significant. They could become shy, and shyness costs.

We'll consider the implications of this personality trait with a two illustrations from the world of business. Then we'll explore some perspectives that one might adopt to support themselves more fully in being affirmative and assertive as they pursue their important dreams.

ROOTS

When we think about shyness per se, we begin to appreciate that it originates from a simple set of beliefs. Or perhaps it would be better to refer to them as a set of judgments. No one can deny that we all have "judgment machines". We take the measure of the people and things around us and internally declare them "good" for us, or "bad" for us. Quite frequently, in self-conscious moments, the shy person turns the focus of this "judgment machine" *on themselves,* and they rarely declare their perceptions to be "good". They will conclude much more commonly, that they are perhaps a bit slow or unimpressive, somewhat uninteresting or unprofessional. They may think they are not well read or sufficiently educated, too fat or thin, too unsophisticated or shabbily dressed, and so on.

Are you shy? It does not matter what the situation may be, or who the people involved are, or what issue is considered ... but deep in your heart ... do you often feel less than adequate? And more importantly, do you come to *believe* that you are less than each situation demands. Do you have a tendency to hold back, to retreat, to avoid the embarrassment of being seen and discovered for what you are? Do you take refuge in anonymity, preferring not be discovered or recognized for what you fail to be? Why would you? What poor self-image.

Shyness is really all about a feeling of inferiority. When people have the "*I'm less than*" feeling, they typically react to it in one of two different ways. Some take those same inferior feelings and beliefs, and try to compensate for them with a mixture of bravado, aggression and loudness. They act up and act out. They seek to draw attention to themselves as if to convince themselves that they are not so inadequate after all. It's a camouflage, a put-on, an attempt to cover up the feelings of insecurity and inferiority. These people seem to be the exact opposite of shy, but yet the underlying feelings are very similar.

Of course, the response that we are most interested in here, is the other typical reaction to the feeling of inferiority or inadequacy. That reaction is spontaneous withdrawal, shyness and sometimes isolation. It's like running away and hiding to avoid being noticed. Such introverts would hate to be the center of attention. The eyes of onlookers radiate beams of rebuke and rejection. And they seem to be everywhere and ever present. They are poised to observe every mistake, every short-coming - real or imaginary - and then rush to criticism and condemnation.

So the shy person chooses to be reserved, to remain obscure, silent and even socially invisible. They affirm nothing, they express no passion, but simply go about their routines quietly and unashamedly. They may even be very good at what they do and very productive, but they cause no stir or fanfare, they lead no chorus and blow no horn. They are retiring, sometimes even to oblivion. They evade cameras, reporters and publicists. They avoid any and all appearances on stage. Could that be you?

When we continue our analysis, it is easy to see the real root cause of shyness. It is a tendency even to *project* on to the people around us the feelings that we ourselves harbor. We first judge ourselves in some way to be inferior, inadequate or vulnerable, and then we project that judgment on to others. We imagine that all the people around us are certain to make the same judgment and to further put us down in the same way. We convince ourselves that they will be intolerant of our weakness and failure. They will know too much about us and will take advantage of that. They will treat us unfairly and with disrespect. So we seek to protect ourselves from all of that. If we do not expose what we are, we can be spared the shame and embarrassment; we can at least keep our sense of privacy, if not pride. We can remain whole. The projection of our own feelings of inadequacy on to the people around us is a very subtle yet powerful influence on how we react in any given situation.

Tied into this imaginary constellation of beliefs, reactions and behaviors that we have just mentioned, is an additional judgment that we usually make at the same time. Just as we judge ourselves to be "less than" (and remember, this "judging" may not even be something that we are consciously aware of), in the same way, we very often make a judgment of the people around us that "*they are more than.*" We imagine that everyone else has it all together. They have mastered the social graces, learned to articulate their ideas with brilliance and have something interesting to contribute. They may even appear larger than life, more gifted than guarded, more gracious than grudging. We exaggerate their attributes and elevate them on to a pedestal in our own minds. They become better, smarter and smoother in our very eyes.

There is another root for this shyness in behavior which derives from a feeling that *we do not deserve the best*, we are unworthy of success. We ought not to have it so good, or to be so acclaimed, or to be under the spotlight. So we back away. We elect not to try for the big one for fear that we may land it safely and rise to stardom. There are things we really want to have, to do or to be, but we dare not ask or seek, for fear that we may find. For if we did ... then what? What if we really exploded? We could not handle the outcome because we were never prepared. We could be overwhelmed and then we would really be shown up for what we really are ... in our minds at least ... a fake, a failure, a foolish wonder.

In summary, if you suffer from acute shyness, you very likely would have an emotional homebase that tends to judge yourself as *"less than"* or inferior, and unworthy of success. You would tend to see others as *"more than"* or superior and you would feel a proclivity to project those beliefs on to the people around you. It's no wonder that some people suffer from a shyness that gets in the way of really squeezing the most out of life. They really want to, but they are shy. Are you?

Psychologists are quick to trace these personality characteristics to childhood experience and development. The shy adult may reflect the influence of domineering or demanding parents. As children they were constantly being assessed, rebuked and even penalized at every turn. Nothing they did was ever quite good enough.

Again, could that be you? Perhaps you were always being compared to someone else - a sibling, neighbor or friend - and you never quite measured up. You may have been "put-down" early when you made an effort to perform or even to please. You could have suffered some major embarrassing moment from which you never quite recovered.

Or you may exhibit some interest, trait or physical characteristic that you have never liked and for which you have often been teased and harassed. It may be your speech pattern, your height or girth, your facial features ... It could be anything. You simply do not approve of something in yourself that you probably can never change.

Some traumatic experience, some emotional or even physical abuse may have left you scarred, apprehensive or even fearful of others. You may have been encouraged to be quiet, to be seen and not heard, to know your place and keep it. That caused you to recoil and you have never unwound since.

Or it could be that you had a mentor, a childhood hero who exhibited a quiet grace, with poise and confidence, which you now imitate.

Whatever the etiology or reason, shy adults can miss out on much that life affords because they fail to assert themselves. They refrain from taking the initiative, from making the first move. They dare little, they attempt less and they conquer nothing at all. To be shy is to choose anonymity and obscurity. At least, on the surface. So the shy person holds back, avoids any activity to make his or her presence conspicuous, hoping that nothing will be expected of them. That way they can never experience **YES!**

FRUITS

To be shy may seem like a benign personality trait, a product of social nurturing and clearly an option that some may even adopt by choice. It may be just a matter of style or preference, an innocent self-expression that defines for them who they really are. There is no law or protocol to determine how one should act in a social setting in terms of taking initiative, making one's presence felt or generally attracting attention. Some choose clearly to be retiring.

Neither is there a precept or condition that one should jump in response to the call of opportunity, or fly whenever the wind blows. It may be preferable to remain on the sidelines, to go about one's own business with a quiet diligence, courting neither credit nor controversy.

But there is indeed much more to being shy than such unassuming nonchalance might suggest. Shy people are in danger of missing out on quite a lot. They can become *losers* in the game of life and pay a high price for this simple personality pattern.

The social order demands that each of us assert some real presence. It is your own responsibility to inhabit your personal space and to take your rightful place. Otherwise you will be invaded and at other times, dismissed.

To illustrate what does happen, let's use a couple examples from the world of business where a habit of shyness might cause the most amount of damage.

Call Reluctance

Let's *role play for a minute.*

Let's assume that you are a sales person who is doing some prospecting by calling up potential customers to see if they have an interest in your product or service. You're sitting at a telephone, you have a list of telephone numbers in front of you and you start to make your way down the list. But assume also that you've always had a problem with shyness, and dialling that first number isn't easy. Such call reluctance is little more than shyness expressed. You've got the telephone in your hands, and you pause. Okay ...

"FREEZE! ... Right there!"

Let's assume that we have such powers to invoke suspended animation and we do just that. We have plenty of time to look into the head of the sales person making those calls, to see what beliefs, judgments and projections we find roaming about in their psyche.

Let's start with personal judgments.

Feelings of inferiority and inadequacy can flood the mind with negative ideas which might go something like this:

- "I'm not sure what I should say when the customer answers.

- If they ask me about my product, I'll be very nervous.

- This product really does have flaws.

- It's priced way too high.

- I'm the last person who should be pretending to be an expert on this product.

- I can't convince anyone of anything. What right do I have to ask this person to buy something I'm not sure I would buy?

- I need more product training.

- I need more sales training.

- I'm the wrong person for this job.

- I should be doing something else.

- I'm an impostor, a fake.

- I'm not a REAL salesperson ..."

Of course, as you probably guessed, it would not be a stretch of the imagination to continue for a couple more pages just elucidating the "less than" judgments you might make about yourself and your product. The longer the calling session goes, the more of these self-judgments you would typically have.

Okay ... but what about the "more than" judgments? What might those be? Well, as call reluctance takes hold of the mind, you surrender to all opposition, you give way to easy rejection. You come to think that the prospect knows more, feels self-satisfied and needs nothing from you. These "more than" judgments may therefore go something like this:

- "This customer probably knows more about the product than I do.
- These people are too important and busy.
- They've probably got the competitors' product.
- They're sure to be smarter than I am, and probably better educated.
- I've got no business calling on these people now.
- They have real lives, full of real accomplishments, but I'm just an impostor ..."

The longer you think about it, the greater the stature that unknown customer continues to assume in your eyes. Before long, you perceive them to be larger than life, bursting with knowledge and experience while resting in comfort and self-sufficiency.

Things are not going good for you as this shy sales-person. But the real damage comes when you take all these negative judgments and start to project them on to the customers you have to call. This is an especially powerful negative influence which feeds the sense of shyness that you would already have. Such projections might sound something like this:

- "The customer doesn't want me interrupting them.
- They don't want this product.
- This service is not what they're looking for.
- They're going to think that I'm stupid and unknowledgeable.
- They're going to realize I don't know what I'm talking about.
- They're going to "find out" that I'm an impostor.
- They are going to be mad at me for wasting their time ..."

That's a litany of projections. You first thought of imaginary ways to disarm yourself, to put yourself down. You then framed those ideas until you judged yourself a failure. You looked up from that defeated plane to see your prospects in an elevated state. They were better than you and had need for neither you yourself, or what you had to offer. Finally, you projected these feelings and judgments on to them until you became a victim of your own imagination as to what their conclusions about you might me.

But think about it, your prospects were totally unaware of your existence or your product. It was all a mind-game going on in the arena of your own perception where you alone defeated yourself. It is a self-fulfilling projection exercise.

Now *back to reality*. That's enough of role-playing.

If you do suffer from shyness at any level at all, the chances are good that you've been through some of that inner dialogue, even if you're not consciously aware of it. And let's face it, if you are really in that mode, and you really do have all of those "less than," and "more than" judgments flowing through your mind, and you really are projecting all those negative assumptions onto other people ... it is no small wonder that you would act "withdrawn" and feel "exposed" or "vulnerable" and put "on the spot".

Sad to say, in some ways, but I'm also happy to declare the truth: *In* this *case, it's all in your mind.*

Job Hunting

Consider another example in business where being shy does cost significantly.

The marketplace is sometimes a rough jungle where only the tough seem to survive. It is not an arena for reticence or restraint. Think of the person in search of a job.

Every day the newspapers in almost any industrialized city are full of 'help wanted' ads. These are jobs being advertised, openings for new employees, opportunities for entrepreneurs. Many of these possibilities for employment require minimal or limited specialized training or experience. They are offered to the public at large to elicit the applications of all interested parties. At a time of high unemployment, it is surprising that each and every able-bodied unemployed person does not scan these listings to find some even remote prospect for employment and follow up with inquiry and application. There are usually openings for sales people in varied fields, unskilled or manual labor, office jobs, in-service training opportunities, lower and middle management positions, plus jobs requiring nothing more than people skills. There are even jobs that demand little more than just physical presence, like security guards, watchmen, cashiers, ticket handlers and so on.

Yet every day there are thousands of unemployed persons in most major cities who do very little to seek a new job. They make no application. Of course there are many reasons for this phenomenon and one must always be sensitive to the emotions and psyche of the displaced persons. Their self-worth is challenged, their ego defeated and their confidence shaken. But imagine what it must mean for the person with a shy personality to be in this rather depressing situation. They scan the job listings but shy away from even the initial inquiry. Even if they spot something interesting, they convince themselves that they have "less than" what that job demands. They would hate to be refused an interview or even worse, to be invited for an interview and maybe, even a follow-up meeting, and then to be rejected. They dread the possibility of being put under the spotlight of the employer's scrutiny, of being questioned about their work history, their values and attitudes. To do that would be to become the center of attention. That's not their bag. They want to avoid such personal encounter and observation.

They imagine that someone else will apply for the same opportunity whose qualifications will be "more than" theirs. So why bother to apply?

Even if they do, they approach the whole process with apprehension. They fail to sell themselves well when they show-up. They dress quite ordinary and shake hands like wet spaghetti. They make little eye contact and initiate no novel items or trends in discussion. They show no distinctiveness. They hold back. They blow the interview.

The next time they get a chance, they project these same impressions and presume the same conclusions. Each interview seems to get more difficult and so the success of each application becomes more remote.

This tendency to be shy or at times modest, can sometimes take a very subtle form. Permit me to give a personal illustration. I am by no means a shy person, at least in my public persona. However, I recall what happened to me when I decided to apply to medical school years ago. The process involved completing standard forms, getting three formal reference letters and then, here's the catch, I had to write a personal letter to the school to introduce myself and share what my reasons and objectives were in pursuing a medical degree.

I did just that, but before I mailed my letter, I showed it to a close lawyer friend whom I have known since childhood. He rebuked me in no uncertain terms. In fact, I think he actually tore up the letter I showed him because he insisted that it was not representative of me in the least. It did not project my accomplishments, my personality, my strengths, my maturity or my goals. I had written a soft, unpretentious letter with no distinctiveness, no flare, no persuasiveness or real conviction. My friend sent me back to the drawing board with the warning that if I were to get past the one in ten chance of admission, I would have to add to my excellent academic record, a projection of style, conviction, warmth and expectation. There was no place for false modesty here.

I heeded the warning and went back to the drawing board. This time I wrote a stunning letter, no less true, but clearly making a strong case for my admission. The difference was like comparing chalk and cheese on a dining table. Needless to say, I was admitted. I tremble to think what could have happened if ...

BOOTS

We have spent some time trying to understand the underlying mechanism or *roots* responsible for debilitating shyness. We just saw how serious the consequences or *fruits* can be. Now we must consider what solutions are possible to overcome it. Three suggestive metaphors come to mind. They illustrate the ability to walk, in turn, in the *boots* of a prospector, a detective and a knight, and thereby show how to work out or work *through* the personal characteristic of shyness.

But before we get to the metaphors, let's first be clear on one thing: if shyness is fundamentally a thinking, judging, believing and projecting problem, then the solution should lie in those very same mental factors. We will have to change our thinking to change our style of living. That's for sure.

Now, let's consider those three important metaphors that will give us some real insight into overcoming the problem of shyness.

Be a Prospector

If you think back to the prospectors who worked in the Klondike early in this century, you would probably have the picture of tough adventurers who braved the rugged wilderness in search of prime turf to stake out. They carefully surveyed the land before them as they went. They searched out the terrain with the best prospects of hidden wealth, natural beauty and land potential. They were eager to lay claim to new territory as their very own. There was wealth and opportunity to be had and they each wanted their piece of the action, the more the better. They were willing to take risks, to work hard and to suffer hardship if necessary. But ultimately they aimed to conquer the frontiers and realize the better life. It was exciting and challenging, and their efforts generally paid off. It was the time of the gold-rush, a time to prove one's worth, where desire, discipline and determination could procure dowry and eventually dollars. Vast and rich regions of the continent invited the daring entrepreneurs to stake out what would be theirs. And brave men and women responded. What a legacy to their credit.

It is this idea of *staking out* your turf that is the most useful part of this metaphor. If you are essentially a shy person, one of the steps you can take to overcome your shyness is to see and believe that you have the right to be here, the right to shape and defend your own ideas and values. You have the right to work towards your most treasured dreams. You have to mentally stake out this prime piece of real estate, which in reality is your own life. You have rights; you have your own tiny part of this planet that you can call your own, and you don't have to apologize to anyone for being here. You're here because you're supposed to be here. No one has the right to take that away from you. No person is preordained to the role of being your master. You can get out of your shell and breathe; you can roam free; you can be all that you were meant to be.

If you are indeed shy, shake off that nagging feeling that you don't belong, that you don't deserve much, and that you don't fit in. Plant your feet firmly on the ground and stake out your claim to your own life ... *That* is ultimately in your control ... and of *that*, you are the master.

So many shy people live in a state of almost continual apology. Therefore, they have to be continually reminded to re-enforce the belief upon themselves that they have the inalienable right to be here. So take this opportunity right now to do some re-enforcing yourself. You need not apologize to anyone for existing. You have just as much right as anyone to the rich rewards that life offers to those people who work energetically and creatively. You need not take a back seat to anyone. You are unique, valuable and irreplaceable. You belong here. You have your place. And the only one who can take it away from you ... is YOU!

Be a Detective

The second metaphor that can be helpful when we are trying to overcome shyness is to become a detective who searches for the facts. Detectives are diligent professionals who are not satisfied with suspicions, impressions and opinions. They are intensely committed to finding out the facts of every case they work on. They leave no stone unturned in search of hard evidence. They follow each lead. They remain alert, perceptive and open. They are slow to come to conclusions for fear that they get sidetracked or overlook important data that affects the case.

Detective work can be intense and obsessive. Sometimes you can have all the pieces to complete the puzzle save one. But that final piece can change everything. So you must persist and follow through until the picture is complete. When all the facts are in, then the picture can be clearly seen and the truth brought to light. One thing we know to be true is that shy people very often have an extremely distorted view of the facts when it comes to their own situation. We have already seen how damaging the perception that we form can be. The truth is that we form such images and conclusions with only a very loose grip on the facts. When we judge ourselves "less than" we are usually reacting to internal feelings and not to the hard facts of the situation.

For any shy person who is trying to overcome the triple negative spiral of irrational beliefs, erratic judgments, and self-condemning projections ... there is nothing more valuable than a prolonged focus on the *real* facts of life. Good detectives turn on the spotlight and bring the truth to light.

Shy people do need a reality filter that gives them a true picture of their situation. You need not be surprised to learn that people are not intently studying your every move; people are not silently thinking all kinds of negative thoughts about you; people are not naturally superior to you in every situation. In fact, you are who you are and what you are, just as other people find themselves to be their unique individual selves. They share the same basic characteristics and needs, and like you, they also know their own strengths and weaknesses. If they accept themselves as they are and therefore can face the world unashamedly, so can you. There's no one else just like you and no one else is as hard on you as you are. So loosen up, lighten up and learn to laugh at the world. The more detective work you do to uncover the true facts of any situation, the less susceptible you are to the irrational processes that determine so much of shy behavior.

Be a Knight

Classical English literature has created a respect and admiration for the old British knight. Whether you find him in Shakespeare or at the round table with King Arthur, you meet a distinguished loyal soldier who with bravery and courage defended the monarch. The knight was a trained fighter, a dependable guard, a proper gentleman. He found his place immortalized in the historic game of chess, a proud protector of the king and queen. He had unusual moves and could pounce upon you when you least expected. He was never to be taken for granted. The tradition is perpetuated today in the "Queen's Honor List" which bestows among other insignia, the Knighthood Bachelor distinction. Such honorable gentlemen are then addressed as *Sir* John Doe which in contemporary terms, acknowledges some distinguished achievement worthy of royal recognition. It is bestowed for excellence in all fields of human endeavor throughout much of the old British Commonwealth. It remains an honor, but it does not connote today the original military significance where men of valor, loyalty and great courage were so honored by the monarch. In any case, it brings one into the spotlight and stimulates effrontery while denoting prominence. It unmasks shyness.

You can be a knight. You can choose to demonstrate bravery, courage and valor and so become a person of honor, worthy of trust, recognition and even distinction. You can choose to act with modesty, style and grace but you can fortify those virtues with confidence, strength and forthrightness. You can choose to put away the shyness that precludes or limits your effectiveness.

One of my favorite quotes, and I wish I could recall who said it, goes like this: "A coward dies a thousand deaths, a brave man dies but once." There is no need to "die" in your mind a thousand times, by imagining horrible consequences and letting your imagination run away from you. Part of the solution to overcoming shyness is just taking steps to simple acts of courage. You need this courage to face your fears and to not be governed by them. Sometimes it really is necessary to just *'feel the fear and do it anyway'*.

A life well-lived requires courage. Let's not deny it or equivocate about it. It is impossible for you to arrange your affairs in such a way that you remove the need to rely on courage to sometimes see you through. After you have staked your claim and tried to see the facts for what they are, you will sometimes have to just courageously take the plunge and then let the chips fall where they may.

Courage, if it teaches us anything, teaches us that sometimes we have to ignore the cost. Instead of focusing on how awkward, vulnerable, or exposed you will *feel* in a given situation, you need to focus on what you are trying to achieve, regardless of the cost. That is one of the central themes of this whole book: life should be full of adventure, meaning, passion, and romance... regardless of the "cost".

So, for those who suffer from shyness ... what can we conclude? Well, as an adult, if you truly suffer from shyness and its consequences, you can now understand that this infliction is a believing, judging, projecting problem that is created in your own mind and that it can be eliminated if you choose. You can start by staking out your own claim to your share of the richness of life and the opportunities available to you in this world. You can truly believe that you have your rights to these benefits without apology. You deserve them. You can then take some careful steps to separate the facts of your situation from the judgments you are inclined to make and try to base your beliefs on facts rather than on such counter-productive and irrational judgments. Finally, you must have the courage to act according to your passions, beliefs and convictions regardless of the costs.

Shyness can be overcome. You can fight first with yourself to overcome your inhibitions. Harness those bold ideas and attitudes and make verbal affirmations as you stake your claims. Then master your body language to communicate an increasing strength and presence wherever you are.

When you do all that, you will start to put debilitating shyness behind you. You will start to look people in the eye. You will start shaking hands with firmness and resolve. You will get out of your shell and investigate the areas of this world that interest and fascinate you. You will stop putting yourself in the back seat. You will start to greet people with enthusiasm. You will start to shed the awful burden of excessive reticence and take your rightful place in the world.

With such effrontery, you are sure to reach for success. You will surmount any challenges that now dog your steps and seize the opportunities at hand. You will at least say **"YES!** *I'll give it a try.*" So do that.

The Evolution of **YES!** *unfolds:*

You must risk participation
as you pursue your dream,
without excuse now,
by making a clear decision
to be
bold enough!

10

Reservation

("YES! I'll give it a try")

By now you would have discovered that the path to
YES! is full of promise and adventure. Surely you have
already overcome many hurdles and the goal now seems close
at hand. You have a healthy self-image. You are eager to
participate, with internal constraint and unconditionally.
Your horizons are inviting and without excuse or delay, you
have decided to venture into a new world. You should be
intrigued and excited about what it could really mean to live a
life that answers **YES!** to all it's possibilities. You could be
one hundred percent positive, passionate and productive as
each day unfolds before you with open arms.

To embrace life is to be embraced by the opportunity
that every day affords, for living **YES!** is a love affair. You
can really see it, now you are almost there. You can sense it
by your anticipatory anxiety. But as tantalizingly close as you
are, something may still be missing.

What may be missing is that your **YES!** might be said with only half-a-heart. That may be one of your final obstacles in the evolution of a resounding **YES!** ... You would never enjoy the fruits of your passion if you only embrace your goals or plan your life with half-a-heart, if you only do your job or love your family with half-a-heart. You would miss the joy of success if you only utilize your talents or lay hold of your dreams with half-a-heart.

Such half-heartedness, if you have not noticed, is also virtually endemic in our society, just like indecision. So often we commit to do something, but we do it tentatively. We go for it, but we are still holding something back. We are still counting the cost, making sure that we do not endanger ourselves. So we say **YES!**, but only to *give it a try*.

This chapter is intended to urge those readers who do everything they do with equivocation, to reconsider the joys awaiting an unabashed, unreserved commitment to **YES!** Just think about what it would mean to take that extra step, and to hold nothing back. What would happen if you used every ounce of God-given talent that you have in the single-minded pursuit of the passion that burns in your heart?

Yes, think about it!

When I think about half-heartedness, again there are three images that come to mind which capture the essence of this personal Phase in the steady progression to truly passionate living. Let's consider each one in turn.

ENGAGE

Imagine ...

You step out your front door on a beautiful Sunday afternoon in the summertime. The sun is still bright in the cloudless sky and you pause to admire your lawn. It is a rich green oasis bordered by perennial shrubs and delicate flowers pruned to perfection. You feel proud as you stand on the front step admiring the sparkling magnificent vehicle sitting in your driveway. On Saturday ... it got the complete works and now it sits there, polished and gleaming, shimmering in the sunlight. Everything about you seems so clean, so crisp and so charmingly manicured. A smile comes to your lips as you cherish your personal toy and status symbol. This day must be full of possibilities. It clearly belongs to you.

You flick an imaginary trace of something off the front hood. It must be an idiosyncrasy of yours. You have microscopic eyes for dust, lint and litter, anywhere and anytime. You eagerly open the door and slide in. This automobile is as meticulously clean on the inside as it is on the outside. You can smell the luxury. You can feel the comfort as you settle in. You revel in it. The mirrors are positioned just right and the driver's seat is adjusted to your satisfaction. You know your car was recently tuned with a complete 64-point diagnostic check. Everything is functioning. You were careful to fill up with high octane gas, and you're now ready for action.

You slide the key in the ignition and gently turn it on. The car roars to life immediately without a sputter or even a hiccup. It purrs like a kitten with a smooth engine sound. You can feel the power of the five litre engine as it idles freely. Now you reach back for your seatbelt and do it up snugly. You are ready, so let's get out of here. You turn the stereo on and music fills the air.

And there you sit, going nowhere. Hour after hour you remain at the command of your ultimate driving machine without ever leaving your driveway. The car idles and sits for hours. You're excited about driving; your fine automobile is truly splendid and the day is even better. But you still go nowhere. As night falls, you run out of gas, the engine stops and you retire to bed with unpleasant dreams. You dream of what could have been.

Why?

The car was never engaged. You neglected to put the car in a moving gear. You failed to make a connection between the drive train and the engine. So you just sat, and waited and pondered, while all the pistons fired away but effected nothing. No motion. No changing scenes. No distance covered. No horizons explored. No scenery enjoyed. No adventure explored. You ended up going nowhere. What a shame! What a waste!

*Now back to where **you** are now.*

Is that a metaphor for life? For some people ... definitely. Even those who get to **YES!** sometimes arrive with such a half-hearted attitude that they are never able to fully engage. They are all set to move but they never actually get their life in gear. Instead, they go through the motions, their engines run idle, they run out of fuel and stagnate, even in high style.

The moral of the story is simple but true. Even when all other circumstances are perfectly arranged, *you cannot drive in neutral*. To get anywhere you have to engage, you have to put the vehicle in gear. You have to leave the driveway and then, and only then, you can begin to enjoy the feel of the road, the panorama of the countryside or the new sights and sounds of your own neighborhood. You don't enjoy them by being comfortably ensconced in the safety of your own driveway. You have to engage. To arrive at any destination you choose, you must drive away from home, from your own comfort zone. You will only go places if you go down the ramp and on to the highway.

This discussion is all about changing gears. It is about putting your life in Drive and starting a new and challenging journey. It is about engaging your resources, your energy and commitment and using them to get everything you can out of the short years you have left on this still green planet. It is about cruising the highway of life without reservation.

Life is not for sitting idly in a comfort zone. No tow

truck will ever come to carry you to success. It's a journey
you must make in the driver's seat. Yes, life is for travelling
to destinations you choose for yourself. Life is for learning
and growing along the way. It is for experimenting, for
taking on new challenges and expanding your horizons. Life
is for loving. It is for becoming. To make any of it happen
you have to change gears and let the journey of your passion
begin. You have to move. And you ought to do it now. Say
YES! Take hold of the gear lever of your own life. That is,
take responsibility, take initiative, take control and engage all
that you are, in pursuit of all that you can be.

What an exciting journey awaits you when you do.

COMMIT

Imagine again ...

You are only nine years old and relatively small of
stature. You are with some of your friends, frolicking away a
summer day outdoors in the ravine close to your house. You
all choose to spend some time looking for frogs and trapping
grasshoppers. When that gets boring, you decide to carve
your name in a rotting tree trunk that is lying by the creek.
That takes no less than twenty minutes of patient work to do
it properly. By the time you finish doing that, the small group
of would-be eagle scouts is feeling pretty daring. Then your

pal Taylor gets an idea. Wouldn't it be neat to try and jump across the creek, from one side to the other?

It does not take long for the others to warm up to that idea, but you are not quite enamored by the proposition. To you the creek looks about a mile wide at the proposed crossing point. Being a near midget does not do a whole lot for your confidence. So you try to divert the troop by suggesting a carefree swing on the tire in your backyard, but no one else responds to that idea. They actually want to jump across. Now.

Since it was Taylor's idea, he goes first. With a long run at full speed and then a good jump, Taylor pedals through the air and hits his mark perfectly as he ends up on the other side of the creek, grinning from ear to ear. Others follow in quick succession. Some seem rehearsed but one or two land in a splash on their little bottoms. But it is all in good fun. They laugh, they cheer, they tease each other. Everyone is having a great time rising to the challenge. That is, everyone except you.

Subconsciously or at least cautiously, you put yourself last in line for the adventure. When your turn finally comes up, you see all your friends joking and laughing on the other side of the creek. But you shiver in your little boots. Your heart races as you break out into a cold sweat. You wish you did not have to do this. It is your small size that's really bothering you. No one lets you forget it. You have speed and stamina but what you need now are the long legs that you never got. You are hesitating but you've got to give it a try. You are on the hot seat. Your friends are all watching and waiting. It is your moment. No one else can do this for you. There's no place to run away and hide.

You gulp once, and start scanning the creek to see if there is a rock that you can use as a half way point, to be different at least. But all you see is rushing, bubbling water.

Finally you back up about twenty to thirty feet and take a tentative run to the bank. But as you do, Taylor screams at you from the other side ...

"STOP! You're going too slowly, you'll never make it. Back up another twenty feet and run as fast as you can."

They have no real idea what you are going through. You think about that advice, but to your nine-year-old brain it makes no sense. You reason with yourself. The faster you run, the quicker you will get to the river bank that is going to be your grave. To go slowly seems much more prudent. Not to go at all would be the wisest thing to do but then you would die from disgrace. You've got to give it a try. If you somehow miss and even die in the process, at least you will die trying.

The creek seems to be getting wider, the water deeper, the current faster, and your short legs shorter. You take a few more tentative runs, and each time you stop at the last second. The jeers and catcalls start on the other side and you're very close to heading back up the hill to go home. But your friends would never forgive or forget this and neither would you.

So you are quite literally stuck. At your young and tender age, you have not yet absorbed one of the most fundamental lessons in life ... *you cannot cross a chasm in two steps.* It is all or nothing. To get across it you need to be travelling as fast as you possibly can. You need to make a single concerted leap to safety and freedom. Timidity, hesitation, and reservation are not much help to a chasm-jumper. They can be quite embarrassing and at times even fatal, depending on the chasm.

Then suddenly, somehow, from somewhere, you resolve to give it a try, in fact, more than a try. You are going to jump across this creek like all the others did-decisively, unequivocally and with no reservation whatsoever. You don't even care anymore where you land, or how you look. It does not matter what the others think. This is for you. It is what you want to do, right here and right now. You're going over.

You step back a few paces, tear swiftly across the brush, gain a good foothold and spring upward and forward like a short Carl Lewis prodigy. You sail through the air with a mixture of trepidation and glee. But you land well past the bank, and feet first. You scream out **"Y-Y-YES!"** Your big friends burst into thunderous applause. That was the jump of the entire day. You've never felt bigger or taller. You are as ecstatic as you've ever been and in one small leap you just became the leader of the pack.

*Now back to where **you** really live.*

Crossing a chasm is an excellent metaphor for **YES!** living. Think about it. We need to know only three things when we cross a chasm: where we are now, where we want to be in future when we land, and the energy and velocity we will need for the leap to get there.

Take the first of these considerations. A lot of people are drifting through life without really knowing where they are. They are not necessarily lost in a complete sense, but large parts of their life are opaque. They cannot see below the surface, behind the veil of what is immediately apparent. It could be for example, that they are going to be laid off in two months and they don't even know it. They just don't realize how tenuous their job situation is. They have a false sense of security. The signs are not obvious.

Or it could be that their spouse has given up on them, yet they are unaware of it. They are making plans for the children and for the future of the family together, unaware that in the short term, there will be upheaval, custody battles and economic hardship. Some signs are there to suggest serious problems in the marriage, but they are grossly under-estimated. They are playing poker.

Or it could be that they are bankrupt without really

understanding their true financial situation. They continue to live well, to spend freely, to make new commitments and to impress others. But in fact, each day they are going deeper and deeper into a debt hole or "money pit" that will eventually swallow them.

Just one more example. They might be in middle age enjoying life and sporting a pack of light filter cigarettes each day. They have not seen a doctor in years since they feel good and look good. But if they knew the truth, a single routine chest x-ray would reveal an isolated nodule. This examination with proper clinical management could save their life. But they refuse to go for a simple check-up. They don't know where they are.

That's the nature of things. A lot of people fall into these and other categories. They are not paying attention, not taking inventory, not having regular check-ups. We need to consistently assess our true state of life's affairs. That is not being paranoid, it is being prudent.

Find out where you are. Take a quiet but brutally honest inventory. Take stock. Review all the important elements of your life--your finances, your career or profession, your relationships, your state of health, your available opportunities, your spiritual inventory--and see where you are. We tend to lie to ourselves a lot and the longer we go without an incisive personal inventory, the bigger and the more frequent the lies become. Deluding other people is immoral, but deluding ourselves is sheer lunacy. Before you start your leap forward into life, you have to know your take off point.

So let's begin to do that.

Stop for a second and think about the area of your life where you most often delude yourself by ignoring, rejecting, or minimizing the truth. Get honest. See what there is to see. Know what there is to know. Human capacity for self-deception is unlimited, but its consequences are also unrelenting.

When was the last time you honestly sat down and constructed a personal financial balance sheet by first listing the value of all of your assets, and then by subtracting all of your liabilities, you discovered your net worth? Maybe now would be a good time to do just that. Get professional help from your bank or a registered financial planner if you need to.

When was the last time you really took a look at which relationships are most important to you and exactly how healthy those relationships are? Take a long look at who are the most important people in your life and how much time you spend with them, how honest the communication is and how openly you share in each other's life. Brutal honesty is an elixir when it comes to understanding self. The more honest we are with ourselves and those close to us, the more we come to understand about ourselves.

How about your career path? Do you have a job that is just that, a job? It's the best thing that you could find. Maybe you even have the bumper sticker that reads 'I owe, I owe ... so off to work I go'. Do you have a profession or a business? You know that your training and skill affords you some choice and flexibility. You take pride in who you are and what you do. Or maybe, as you read this book, you are in transition. Perhaps career disturbed? Unemployed? Underemployed? Whatever your situation, have you recently assessed where you are and what you are doing for most of your waking life? I came to realize years ago that we will each spend two-thirds of our life doing only two things ... working and sleeping. I therefore determined that there are at least two things I must always enjoy ... yes, revel in ... a hard day's work and a good night's sleep. How about you?

And need I ask, when was the last time you had a medical examination? Prudence suggests that at least every one or two years you should visit your family doctor for a routine periodic health and wellness survey. A regular periodic health assessment can focus on preventative health care that can save years of morbidity and suffering, if not life itself. It is proactive but critical. Need I say more? Again, a word to the wise is always sufficient.

Know where you are!

The second thing you have to know when you jump that chasm into life and into the future is where you are going. In your own life, what is it that represents the other side of the chasm? You need to know where you are going, specifically and in detail. It has been said before, but it bears repetition, 'it is impossible to reach your dreams in life if you don't know what they are.'

You've heard the adage, 'If you don't know where you are going, you are bound to end up somewhere else'. Don't be like the proverbial fellow who set out not knowing where he was going. When he arrived he did not know where he was. Finally, when he returned he did not know where he had gone.

I once worked for a large organization specializing in photocopying equipment. It's a fine company and they treat their employees well. But I can remember the day I observed that if everything went well for me in my research position, the best I could look forward to was my own boss's job. Then I concluded that I did not want his job. At that moment, I knew in my heart at least, that my service in that place was short term. May I suggest for your consideration that if you don't want the next promotion where you are, you had better be looking around.

In my practice I counsel many a victim of a soured relationship. After years of devotion, open communication and hope of lasting union, the curtain comes down. Usually the male partner is off to seek greener pastures and the unfortunate companion is left alone - bruised and often used. I now argue that young women in particular who know that intimate relationships are on certain dead-end courses, going absolutely nowhere sooner or later, would be wise to anticipate their future and make their move ... the sooner, the better. They can spare themselves the pain, the rejection and the regrets.

It is always a good time to review one's goals. It permits you to stay on course. So many people drift away from their early destination by simple carelessness and at times, recklessness. They are blown about by circumstances and show nothing but passive indifference until they near the end. Then comes the rude awakening as they discover they missed out on life's best, and sometimes on life itself.

How about you? Can you see across your chasm of opportunity where some challenge invites you? Is that resonating with your own passion and your highest intentions for yourself? If you choose to cross over, you had better approve of where you are going to land. So set your course by conscious choice.

How about your finances? When I was only twenty-four and just finishing grad school, I was invited to participate in a real estate venture. I could not be bothered. I was more interested in research papers and teaching positions. Even when it came time to purchase our first home, I did not anticipate real estate market trends. I was not alert and did not perceive where my finances were headed. I later learned. Fortunately, not too much later. I was *only* set back about twenty thousand dollars on my first home purchase.

Talk to any financial planner. The vast majority of even professional types do not really know where they are heading in monetary terms. Short term, medium or long term projections are neglected and even high-income earners with poor investment portfolios and inadequate cash flow constraints, usually seek help only in desperation. Baby boomers are said to be now scrambling for retirement options and strategies.

Do you know where you are going financially?

Goals, goals, goals ... we were meant to have them. Do you have your own? As you look off into the future, can you see where you are headed? Nothing in the world can substitute for that sense of direction. Right now I am thirty-seven thousand feet up in the air looking down on snow-capped mountains in the Northwest United States but I am relaxed. This plane is going south and east to Dallas, Texas. The pilot knows this and so do I. When we land, I'm off to speak to a group of four hundred people at the Arlington Marriott Hotel on Convention Center Drive. When I get into my limousine, I know what I'm going to tell the driver. I know exactly where I'm going. So I'm relaxed. I'm focused.

But that's just one trip. Every day, we are individually challenged to know where we are and where we are going. If we don't we could be anywhere, and end up going nowhere, or just drift to somewhere else that we did not plan. So forgive me if I need to ask the question again. Do you know where you are going--today, tomorrow, next year, in five years? What a vital question and so few really have the answer. Do you?

Know where you are!

Know where you want to be!

Now for the leap. Now for that brisk run that we take to prepare for our jump. We want to run as fast as our legs can carry us. Forget about anything half-way. We can't shuffle or stroll our way to success. We can't tap dance across the chasm to land in our dream by equivocating, hesitating and agonizing over every detail. We have to take off and fly. **YES!** means **YES!** and nothing less.

It is as simple as crossing the street. Once we leave the curb, our destination is the opposite corner. We have no interest in hanging out in the middle of the intersection. That's a sure way to get run over. It is as simple as stealing second base. Once we take off we are committed, we dig in and go as fast as we can. No trepidation. No weighing the risks. Once we leave our base, we are either safe or out at the next. But we are committed. It is as simple as that pilot thundering down the runway about to take off. Once the aircraft has reached near maximum speed and the nose is about to lift off the ground he or she is committed. It is all or nothing. Win or lose. Success or failure. There is a point of no return.

Those stakes are too high for many people who believe that prudence and caution are the most intelligent attitudes to have in pursuing their goals. Their strategy is to avoid the big mistake. Not only do they spend a lot of time, figuratively speaking, in the driveway with the engine idling, but they also look to cross the chasms of life in two steps, trying to find a way that they can muddle through to success.

But that's not the way it works. You must muster every ounce of energy, every breath of life, every drop of commitment you can. You must bring them all together and make a mad passionate dash for your dreams, committed to making the leap, to feeling the solid ground of success on the other side. Throwing caution to the wind, you must stand ready to succeed or fail, with your whole self committed to the enterprise at hand. I never tire of Robert Schueller's observation that "it is better to be a failure attempting something than to be a big success at doing nothing".

Where do you stand? Are you absolutely, totally committed to your dreams, allowing nothing and no one to stand in your way? That's what living the exclamation of **YES!** really takes. And that is when the real fun begins.

> *Know where you are!*
> *Know where you want to be!*
> *Make one concerted leap to get there!*

HEART AND SOUL

Imagine just one more time ...

The final image that puts this whole issue in perspective is a medical scenario.

The ambulance pulls up on the exclusive driveway with sirens going, lights flashing and the paramedics sweating, but busy at what they do best. A middle aged man is quickly wheeled into the emergency ward on a stretcher. He has complained of severe chest pains and now with intravenous lines and oxygen support, he is promptly moved into the coronary care unit. The resuscitation team is naturally prepared for the admission and they immediately go to work. After the doctors manage to stabilize the patient and complete a cardiac work up, they determine that he has had a heart attack.

But, fortunately for this poor fellow, the artery that was blocked off was on the *back* of his heart. He lost some limited muscle cells on the posterior wall of his right ventricle and he now shows some dyskinetic movement on the echocardiogram. But that is not the whole picture. The wise cardiologist later orders a coronary angiogram that shows some significant blockage in the important branch of the main coronary artery on the front of the heart. In his case, coronary balloon angioplasty is not an indicated clinical option. He needs an even more aggressive response. So the patient is later booked for surgery.

He must have a by-pass procedure soon. If he does not and the coronary flow is compromised again, he is at risk of serious damage to his most important left ventricle. That might well be fatal. Why? *You cannot survive on half-a-heart.* In fact, if any half of the heart dies-- top or bottom, front, back or either side--it is 'good night'.

The heart is an amazing essential organ. It functions as a single unit with cooperation and coordination of all its parts. Just imagine what constitutes a single heartbeat. A spontaneous change in critical cardiac cells creates an electrical impulse that flows along a pathway of nerves. These nerves innervate cardiac muscle cells, causing them to contract, which forces the blood past opening valves while others remain closed. The nerve impulse subsides, the muscles relax, the valves alternately close and open. The nerve cells recharge and the process starts all over again. In less than a second, the heart acts in concert to reiterate the cycle.

But, wonder of wonders: it needs oxygen derived from coronary blood flow around the heart to keep it going. It takes a whole heart to maintain a whole life. No less.

This patient does very well. Like the other thousands of similar patients who have the cabbage '(CABG)[1] procedure

---

1. Coronary Artery bypass graft.

each year, he goes home in a week or two, recuperates well and in a few months is back to his normal life with good prognosis, at least for the next decade or so. But he must be followed regularly with careful medical surveillance.

*Now back to **your** heart condition.*

Consider the implications which go beyond the fist-size muscle that beats regularly within the human chest. That is a life generator, a life saver. But like the ancient Greeks, the *heart* means much more than the cardiac pump which they hardly understood. The heart is really the seat of human passion, the fountain of desire. It is the center from which we derive our strongest emotions and most compelling attitudes. It generates love, courage, commitment, hope, compassion, enthusiasm, to mention but a few of life's richest and best qualities.

What is true of that muscle in the bosom is also true of the muscle of the soul that we also call the heart. You cannot *live* with only half a heart. You need your whole heart. You cannot truly *love* with only half a heart ... you need your whole heart. You cannot even *laugh* or enjoy the very best that life has to offer if you have but half a heart.

In the same way that your body needs your whole heart organ to pump blood through your circulatory system, your success or enjoyment of life also requires a whole heart to pump courage into your soul, to give commitment to your passions, to infuse unconditional love into all your relationships. It just cannot be done with half a heart. Anyone who is not pouring their whole life into their innate passions is not really living it *all* or perhaps even *living* at all.

This is such a key idea in saying **YES!** to life. To give life the old schoolboy's try is not living. That is existing. It is passing the time. You must find something you can willingly put your whole heart and soul into. It is the real secret to a satisfying life.

So many count the cost. They hold back. They don't commit. They choose to wait and see. But what exactly are they waiting for? Half-hearted efforts produce half-hearted results.   Reasonable efforts produce reasonable results. Massive efforts produce massive results. There is absolutely nothing to wait for. Take the life that was given to you and spend it on a great enterprise, spend it on something you cherish, spend it on someone you love, spend it on your life's passion. But spend it.

Life is so much more exciting, passionate and charged with meaning when we have ultimate beliefs that we would live and die for. They give us a wonderful clarity of living. They lift us out of what I call the *Four Seas* (4**C**'s) that govern our lives. The typical person in our age lives a life that is either Calculated, Conditional, Compromised, or Contained. And they suffer for it. They drift on those high seas, buffeted by the waves and always at risk.

Calculated. We all know this person. They live by their brain, carefully calculating each advantage, cautiously weighing each alternative, choosing the option that maximizes the potential return in any given situation. They are the ones who make sure the bill is evenly split to the last penny when they eat out with friends. For them, rationalism is the highest good. There are no absolutes, only situational advantages. Life is a game of chess. There is no better good than simply coming out of every transaction ahead of their opponent. A calculated life produces predictable results that may be materially rewarding but leave the heart and soul barren. This person may have a big head but only a small heart to share, small arms to extend to hug the world and small feet to move around. Reason has its place for sure, but it must be energized by passion. The heart supplies the brain and not vice versa.

Conditional. The conditional person is the "IF" person. We met them in Phase Four earlier. They are perfectly prepared to say **YES!** to life if everything is in its place. They will act if they get cooperation from their spouse. They will begin if they get the education they think they need. They will try if they get the job promotions that they deserve. For them life is one long list of "IF's". Their favorite answer is, "It all depends". So they hold back, they wait, they vacillate, they rely on circumstance. In the end, they only succeed if everything falls into place. But things only fall into place if they have heart and soul. So they hardly find peace of heart or joy of soul.

Compromised. This is the person who offers a **YES!** to life that is negotiable. They can make no clear and firm decision. Everything must be qualified. All choices and actions must be negotiated. They follow the crowd as they study the polls. When trouble begins to cloud the horizon, their dream or goal is the first thing to be compromised. Life might be tough on them, but in the end they get more than they give. Equivocation is their primary response to opportunity. They will stoop to conquer, do anything to please and join in any fashion parade. They may finish with praise but never with pride. They lack both fortitude and integrity.

Contained. These are the folks who have never, not even once, pulled out the throttle all the way. They live life on fractional power. They never give themselves to any project, any relationship or any goal with complete and utter abandon. They may have said **YES!** to life, but their yes is highly contained. For some reason they just cannot let go. They are in a box that was constructed by their own hand. They have little idea of what their true limits are. They will bury their talent and take comfort in knowing that they did not fail often. What poor stewards of opportunity!

This is all about letting go. Just go. Don't calculate. Don't hold back your heart and soul. Don't buy into cynicism. Don't sell out to half-heartedness. Just go! Go! And that merges you into traffic. Follow on.

TRAFFIC LIGHTS

Think of something as simple and ubiquitous as a traffic light. In 1923 an Afro-American named Garrett A. Morgan, invented the first automatic traffic signal. He witnessed a crash between an automobile and a horse-drawn carriage. The person in the car was knocked unconscious, the people were thrown from the carriage and the horse had to be shot. The General Electric Co. paid him $40,000 for his invention. Imagine that.

This colorful gadget was the first to regulate traffic flow in an orderly but efficient manner. But Morgan had invented more than just a traffic light. He had capitalized on something much more valuable. It encoded a universal principle about human dynamics that has remained obscure. So let me explain.

Traffic lights are universal. You now find them everywhere in every country of the world. And yet despite all the advancements of modern technology, with computers and electronic controls, the basic traffic light system has never been improved. Rush hour traffic in large modern cities can have up to four thousand cars through a major intersection in a single hour with one single light at each corner of a 4-way stop. Multiple crossings at complex intersections where two or six roads meet still function with the same basic triple lights. That's because there is something fundamental here. The lights are all the same with three basic colors of red, amber and green. Simple little traffic lights they are, but they tell us a story that we ought to pay attention to very closely.

We all know that each of the colors has a clearly defined meaning.

Red means stop. Stand still. Don't move. Stay there. Go nowhere. Do nothing. Relax. Attempt nothing. Change nothing. Just be there. As long as that light remains red, no one can judge you wrong if you just freeze.

Amber implies that you can move forward if safe to do so. Exercise caution. Look around you and behind you. Listen for sounds. Watch for all other instructions. Above all, be careful. Move, but not too fast now. Take your time. Easy does it. Be cool. No rush. Speed is no virtue. Proceed slowly ... with caution ... and don't get excited. Be prepared to stop at a moment's notice. So don't give your all. Hold back. Be restrained. Watch out, things could get dangerous.

Green says go. Everything is clear, so move ahead. Keep your eyes on the road, your hands on the wheel and put your foot down on the pedal. Take off your brake. Just follow the road. Enjoy the ride.

Now for the magic of truth. Each of these lights defines a state of human life and endeavor. At any given moment you are choosing to express your life as if faced by a red, amber or green light. In any dimension of your existence you can evaluate if you are standing still, going nowhere, and making no progress. You are then simply failing to grow or even to change. That's your red light staring at you. It is in other words, a state of stagnation, status quo.

Otherwise, you are advancing slowly and cautiously, making minor gains at this or that activity, or else developing slowly along a path of personal growth. But it's all calculated, conditional, compromised and contained. That's amber right before your very eyes if you can see.

And then there's green, where life is open season. You are moving along, excited, energized, engaging all your reserves and resources to become the best that you can be. You are making progress along several lines, moving from one victory to another. You see a clear path up ahead in the direction of your goals and you are thrilled to be on the road. It is a journey of a lifetime, with nothing but the wind and the bumps in the road to contend with. But that's no big problem really, because the green light signals you to keep moving ahead. It is safe to go forward. Let your engines roar and your hair blow in the wind, only remain on high alert.

Now that you appreciate the meaning of these basic color signals, let's consider the *sequence*. What is the order? Say them. You probably did like most people, you said red -

amber - green. But ah? That's a big mistake. That is never
the order of traffic lights. Not the time sequence. The true
sequence is always red, then green, then amber.

What a difference that makes and what a fundamental
precept it underscores about life in the real world. Keep in
mind, if there was any other sequence to improve the flow of
human traffic, by now somebody somewhere would have
invented it or demonstrated it. After all the sophistication of
modern automobiles, and after all the advances in computer
technology, the sequence of the simple traffic lights in New
York, Paris, Tokyo, Toronto, Lagos or Melbourne is still

red - green - amber.

That sequence does provide valuable insight into
human dynamics. It is most important. Yet millions of
drivers the world over never see this application to their daily
lives.   We see it every day when we drive, but we ignore it
in our life ... the fact that green *follows* red.

Green *always* follows red.

What that implies in life's practical terms is that
whenever you find that you are facing a red light--that is, at a
stand still, at their wit's end, frustrated, extended to the limit,
going nowhere--it is imperative that you do *not* move with
great caution (amber) but that you just get up and go. You
must pull out the stops, take your foot off the brakes and
apply the fuel of your passion to generate action. Dare to be
daring, attempt something new. Move, don't just stand there,
go for it (green). Just go!

Most of us unconsciously live our life on amber. We are cautious, contained, calculating and compromised. We proceed with caution, waiting for the right time to go or to really accelerate. And ironically, amber is the most dangerous zone. That is when most accidents occur at traffic intersections. It is a time of indecision, apprehension, temptation, presumption, and even recklessness. All of that adds up to mishaps waiting to happen.

But as the traffic light reminds us dozens of times a day, amber does not precede green, **amber precedes red**.

Just think. You need that time for transition. You should not quit school because you messed up one exam. It is generally foolish to walk out of a marriage impulsively before attempts at communication, consultation and counseling. To resign from a job in the heat of an argument could prove very costly in the morning. To close down a business at the end of a single bad day or month is usually lunacy.

In each typical case, that would be equivalent to slamming the brakes down hard while moving at a good speed. First, you should slow down and *then* if necessary, apply the brakes. Caution is advisable before you *stop*, NOT before you *start*.

Life changes are regulated just like a traffic light.

If you are stopped, the next step is to just go. Go. Green is for go. Go. Go! GO! Just **GO!** Don't think about it. Don't agonize. Don't equivocate. Just GO! **Just GO!**

But if you are moving, avoid slamming your brakes down. Hesitate, calculate, speculate ... and then come to a stop only if you must. In other words, allow an interval of time to elapse, a transition period, before you get out, not get in ... before you get off, not get on ... before you turn it off, not turn it on. Be doubting before you quit in failure, but be daring in your quest for success. That's wisdom at work.

Reflect on the next traffic light you see.

Are you ready for the next *challenge*?

*   *   *

The Evolution of **YES!** *unfolds:*

You must risk participation
as you pursue your dream,
without excuse now,
by making a clear decision
to be bold enough and
commit!

11

Challenge

("YES!! I'll do my best")

You have cultivated a healthy self-image and found your own place in the world. You have taken the risk of entering into a life of passion with positive expectations and even a sense of urgency. You are clear in your mind about where you're going and what you want to do. You are in Drive, with a keen eye on the road ahead. In fact, you have come a long way. It has taken a big effort on your part. And you are doing just fine. When you examine or assess your situation, you can see tangible evidence of accomplishment all around you. Congratulations on your success.

Success in life is simple but not easy. You know that it does require consistent self-discipline, a daily struggle to keep your chin up and to put your best foot forward. With each sunrise, you must be optimistic, assume your responsibilities and give of your talents uncompromisingly. Like Wall Street traders, you must carefully invest your best blue-chip commodities of time, thought and the energy that you have been loaned, to generate a good return.

The fact that you are now taking such responsibility seriously is more than a feather in your cap. It is positive proof that you are one of the ten percent of people who wake up facing the sunrise and deserve to be rewarded for helping the other ninety percent to roll over and see the light. If we are truly talking about you, then take a bow, help yourself to a bouquet and go to the bank to collect, for you really do deserve it. You already stand out above the crowd.

But just to make sure that you do see yourself, at least to some extent, in this self-selected group of passionate livers (not lovers!), take a moment to review quickly some major components of your life.

How about your relationships? In the end, perhaps that is all that really matters. How good are yours? I'll guess that most of them are fine. You respect the people in your family and you value them. And that's not just empty talk. You can point to many situations where concern for the welfare of your spouse or your children, has made the big difference in how you chose to act in a given situation. That's because you care, you really do, and you're not afraid to show it. No wonder you hug so much. That too is a measure of passionate living. Don't short-change yourself. Give an extra hug today.

How about your career? I'll bet that you take your job seriously, and you conduct yourself in a very professional way. Almost any job in this day and age requires patience, diligence, perseverance and a high tolerance for handling stress. But you're not just hanging in, you're contributing. You're part of a team. Your ideas are probably being used and you're setting an example for the people around you. When it comes to daily application, you're front and center. As for enthusiasm, you probably overflow. You're always extending your reach, trying new techniques and new perspectives to get the job done more smoothly and effectively. You have a real 'passion for excellence'.

When it comes to extra-curricular activities, I'll bet that is where you really excel. Life is much more than work. Aren't you the one who so religiously devotes their time to the latest community initiative? Maybe you are nearing retirement and all that really matters now is what you can give to others to make a difference in the world. You have matured. You've got a sense of purpose and the vision to see all things in perspective. Maybe you have school age children and you are active in the parent-teacher association fighting for a zero-tolerance policy on drugs. Or perhaps you coach little league baseball or sing lustily in a barbershop chorus. You could be committed to the environment and be leading a group to promote the 3 R's in your local community: reduce, re-use, recycle. You are making a difference.

Maybe you don't like politics but you are aware of the issues and you have convictions and values when it comes to civic responsibility. If you are college age, you're probably fighting for social justice, or volunteering for the cancer society, or you're off to the Third World to mix business with pleasure. As a blue collar worker, on or off the assembly line, your cheerful spirit and reliability make you a natural union steward. You are fighting for a cause you believe in. You're no hermit, and whatever gifts you have, you are more than happy to share them with the people around you.

That could indeed be you alright. You've taken the measure of your powers, learned your place in the world and what things in it can really serve you even as you serve others.

Yes, the truth is that you are giving life a good run. You've got lots to be proud of and you're doing your part to make this little green ball a better place. You are giving your best, doing all you can do and really trying to succeed. That's exactly what you promised yourself.

But could it be that despite your best efforts, you are still not making the grade. *You've done your best but your best is still not good enough.* You still seem to fall short of your own expectations. You know that there is more, much more for you to realize.

So now what?

Surely all is not lost. Good guys do deserve to win. Or do they? Even when they do not measure up? Is life some process of consolation where there are prizes for all those who ran as far or as fast as they could? Or are we called to equip ourselves, to train and to get better?

BETTER THAN BEST

Let's ask again. What happens when you've done your best and your best is just not good enough? You try hard, giving to life all you've got, but you keep coming up shorthanded. You dive with passion into the mainstream but somehow you keep emerging on the sidelines. You try catching some wave of success that will lead on to fortune but you never seem to be in the right place at the right time. You've wrestled with a problem to the point of frustration, if not exhaustion, and the same challenge is staring you in the face. When will relief come into view? Is the promised land only a promise, or is it real estate? Is this all there is? You gave it all, to get it all, but you still don't quite have that elusive dream that will fulfill your passion.

That's exactly where a lot of good people find themselves. Oh, do they try hard! When things get tough, they prove they are tough because they get going. They do believe that the harder they work, the luckier they'll get. The more they give, the more they will deserve to win. So they work harder still, they give even more of themselves. They have never been slacking or slouching, they've been giving it everything they've got for a long time now, but somehow it just isn't good enough. They are not getting the results they anticipated or enjoying the degree of success they would like.

What do you do now? What do you do when your best is just *not good enough*? Let us venture to take a look at what you can do when you've already done everything and you still fall short.

When you speak with people as much as I do, you find there is no shortage of people who will tell you quite contentedly that they are 'doing okay' and so, 'thank you very much'. They insist that things are good, they're doing as well as can be expected. These people are proud of their accomplishments, with very good reason, because they do have something to show for their effort. But they may never have fulfilled their passion, never known the productivity of which they are capable and so failed to make the difference in the world which they are called to make.

Don't get it wrong. Contentment is a virtue. There is a state of mind and heart that rests, almost stress-free, accepting the course of life with all its paradox, injustice, frustration and the Law of Murphy. To demand too much of yourself is to defeat your purpose and to negate all noble effort and the striving to succeed. To be too introspective and to take yourself too seriously is to become anxious, paranoid and self-deprecating to the point that you would kill the joy, the spontaneity and all the juicy fruits of passion. You must find the ability to laugh at the world, to humor yourself and to let go. It is the same ability to live in the present.

To truly revel in the moment is to hold everything lightly in the palm, to weigh all things in the mind as scales of dust and to cherish with pride in the heart, what is now and what will always remain.

But having said all that, to move forward with any expectation and dignity, you must hold some disdain for the present state of things, some dissatisfaction with present levels of performance and some discomfort with the inertia of stagnation.

The creation of time forces you to advance forward to inhabit the next moment. The creation of space challenges you to expand and explore the possibilities of growth. And the creation of consciousness compels you to anticipate and accept the inevitability of change.

All living things are constantly changing. You are either getting better or you are getting worse. You cannot elect to change or not to change. You can only choose the direction of change. We cannot, we must not, we will not stand still. Never!

Certainly you aren't just called to be *good*. You aren't even called to be *better*. You are called to be *the best* ... to be the very best that you can be. Therefore it is time to raise the bar, time to shake off any lukewarm response you have to your gifts, talents and opportunities, and to really see what you are made of. There is no way to subject yourself to the test, to truly find yourself, until you refuse to be satisfied with the *good* and take on the challenge of being the *best*. And when your best is still inadequate, there remains a further challenge. Follow closely.

So what do you do when your best is not good enough? You guessed it... You get better. You change, you grow. You become something else, something more than what you've known until now. You set higher standards. You reach deeper into the source of your strength as you reject mediocrity and all it stands for. You must continue to get better all the time.

'Better' is the bridge between good and best,
but it also connects your personal best
with everything else.

When your best is not good enough, you have to change. It is just that simple. When you are doing well, when everything is going "good" even by objective standards, that is when the real job begins. You have to change your thinking, change your attitude, change your goals, change your plan, change your work habits and change your self-image, even then. It is time to change, for change is not really an option. It is inevitable. Only the direction you can choose.

If we take a religious perspective, we might say now is the time to be reborn, to be renewed, to be transformed through the power of a changed mind. Human beings were not designed and created to be trapped in a cycle of negative and unproductive attitudes which cramp their exposure and experience. That is not a true reflection of human capacity. That is not why we are here. We are born to grow and to become more and more like what the Creator intended.

Stop selling yourself short. There is so much more out there for you to have, to do and to be. So much more. Break through the barriers and remove the shackles. Go all the way. Become an extremist when it comes to your dream. Accept no compromises. There is an overflowing abundance of good things and worthy tasks that are available, if only you become "unrealistic" enough to fill your mind and heart with their achievement. Go ahead, raise the bar; but at the same time, raise your efforts; raise your commitment; raise your expectations; raise your spirit to strive and struggle for every one of them.

"How?", you ask.

When your best is not good enough, first you need to *re-examine your vital signs.*

RE-EXAMINE YOUR VITAL SIGNS

Medically speaking, as you may have learned in any basic first-aid course, the four vital signs are simply as follows: pulse, temperature, blood pressure, and respiration. They are called 'vital' because they are critical indicators of one's state of health or even life itself. They are 'signs' because they are observable and not just subjective impressions. In any emergency ward or hospital room, or on a normal day in the doctor's office, or whenever some "patient" needs immediate assessment, these four signs are the vital parameters that, at a glance, give indication of the patient's true condition. But they could indicate something else. Beyond the physical state of the body, they could relate directly to life itself.

Pulse

A normally healthy pulse is regular, at about seventy two beats per minute. It is strong and smooth on the upstroke and the downstroke. It is a true vital sign, a sign of both life and health. Healing art practitioners have become so skilled at monitoring this vital sign that in some parts of the world, the practice of pulse diagnosis has become a widespread and trusted clinical methodology. Some would insist that such a technique is art and not science but in a technological age, much has been lost through neglect of the *art* of medicine. But that is for another forum.

By analogy, whatever endeavor you are engaged in usually involves the consistent performance of *routine activities* which constitute its life blood. It is these same essential elements that, taken together, will produce the results you seek. Your achievement pulse then, is a measure of the frequency with which you are actually engaged in doing the routine things that lead to success in your chosen enterprise.

For someone in sales, for example, that would be the frequency of sales calls or customer contacts. It is obvious that sales is entirely a numbers game. It is governed by *the Law of Averages: Action produces results, massive action produces massive results, and the success ratio can be changed.* The pulse of a salesman therefore would simply be a numerical measure of his client contacts and his closing ratio.

For a student, it would obviously be the measure of hours spent in effective study on a daily or weekly basis. For a pianist or figure skater, it would be a measure of the hours spent effectively rehearsing their skills. For a doctor, it would be the frequency of patient contact, or of continuing education to maintain and upgrade current knowledge and skills. For a pilot it would be flying time. For a young mother, it would be contact hours with her pre-school children. For a minister, this might be the daily devotional time in his study. For a blue-collar worker, it would be the time spent in self-enrichment after he or she leaves the assembly line. What is it for you?

In a word, you can measure how you are given to doing, day in and day out, the routine things that pertain to your fulfillment and success. A weak or absent pulse is a definite emergency.

Take time to identify your own pulse. What are the critical activities in your daily schedule that you need to do on a consistent basis to achieve your desired results? They may be even mundane and undesirable, but they alone can make the difference between ultimate success and failure. Monitor your pulse, especially when you feel you've done your best and your best is not good enough.

Temperature

Normal body temperature is $98.4°F$ $(37°C)$. By different physiological processes, the human body is able to maintain a stable equilibrium called homeostasis. In a wide range of external temperatures, the body adapts to maintain near normal temperatures for survival. Generally, it is higher than the surroundings. Changes in body temperature are strongly suggestive of illness or disease, especially infection and cardiovascular problems, among others.

By analogy, the temperature of your life is a measure of the state or quality of your *feelings.* That might be reflected in your mood or affect, as well as in your temperament and personality. In this regard, there is a widespread diversity of the human condition.

On one extreme, it is possible to be cold and suffer from **hypothermia.** This describes the person who is feeling low, depressed, bored, nonchalant, indifferent, demotivated, with little or no passion, low energy and not much to offer the world. To be in their presence is to feel weighed down, dragged, drained and sometimes even drowned. Their words are few, their smile forgotten, their movements fidgeting and their spirit fragile. They continue to exist but they are unplugged from any source of heat, energy or vitality. Severe hypothermia is a life threatening condition.

In contrast and at the other extreme, it is possible to be hot with **fever.** This describes the person who is feeling agitated, hot-under-the-collar. They are mad with someone or angry about some situation which they usually cannot change. They are critical and complain to everybody about everything. These people are upset and they show it. They are often red in the face, raising their voices and 'carrying-on', as it were. At other times, they are biting their lips, clenching their fists, shaking or shifting nervously. In either case it does not take much to sense their mood or disposition. This is the emotionally febrile condition which might suggest that they have been invaded by infectious ideas or attitudes, or that there is some systemic malfunction in their psyche that needs to be addressed.

Between these polar extremes is the normal healthy emotional state where warm feelings flood the soul. These are soft, uplifting and life sustaining emotions that make life full of passion, full of power and full of productivity. Consider the value of feelings like confidence, compassion and courage, or of enthusiasm and excitement, of commitment and cooperation. Warm feelings such as these brighten the day, permeate a life and radiate warmth and blessing to others.

What about you? What are your feelings like? What can you discern from this vital sign in your own life? Are you cold or hot, or are you warm with feelings that would make you justifiably proud? Have you learned to be the master of all your emotions, detached from the turbulent vicissitudes of life, or are you riding an emotional roller-coaster that chokes the possibilities of any given day? Have you learned to laugh at yourself and the world, not taking yourself too seriously but keeping all things in balanced perspective?

If you are too cold, you need to rekindle your passion and rediscover the fire of some chosen dream to warm your heart and soul. If you are too hot, you need to stand back from the heat of your situation. Pause and reflect on who you are, on what you ultimately want, on what then is really important and on how to create cooling, effective change. You gain nothing by blowing your top and lashing out. Fight only against the truly negative forces of opposition, to restore your own warm feelings and gain all the benefits of emotional homeostasis. Live above the level of your surroundings.

Blood Pressure

The measurement of blood pressure is routine in every emergency department and hospital ward. In the family doctor's office it is a vital sign of hypertension, a widespread chronic disease in most Western societies, with potentially damaging consequences. The two key parameters are the systolic and diastolic pressures. The *systolic* pressure is the upper pressure and measures the peak force of shear flow generated by cardiac contractility and against systemic vascular resistance. The *diastolic* pressure is the opposite and lower pressure that results from the relaxation of the heart near the end of the cardiac ejection and reflects the volume of blood in the body. In more simple terms (and at the risk of oversimplification), the blood pressure reflects the contractility or force of contraction of the heart, the muscular tone of blood vessel walls, and the blood volume. The normal blood pressure for a young healthy person is 120:80 in units of millimeters of mercury. Usually there is a tolerance of 20 mm systolic and 10 mm diastolic, before there is clinical concern. Marked or rapid changes in the typical values for any given person also have clinical significance.

By analogy, the *life pressure* may be regarded as a measure of passion (systolic) and productivity (diastolic). The normal cycle begins with the burning desire to have, to do or to be. This constrains all the personal activity and brings concerted effort to bear in pursuit of some chosen goal. Your passion is your drive. As you apply yourself, your productivity is maintained.

There are two main dangers: hypotension, or low blood pressure, and hypertension or high blood pressure. **Hypotension** leads to a clinical condition called 'shock' which represents poor or inadequate perfusion of essential organs like the brain, the kidneys and the gut including the liver and pancreas. When your passion subsides there is a danger that your *life* could go into shock with threatening consequences. All the essential components of life are then at risk. It is your passion, from your instinct for survival, up to and including your love of life, which drives most of your thinking and behavior. You must guard and nourish the passionate core of your being. Feed it with values and vision, through exposure and exercises of the imagination, and by association with others of like disposition.

The opposite extreme is **hypertension**, or high blood pressure. It is just as serious and much more common. This is the person who has strong passions that are undesirable and often debilitating, instead of healthy and life-affirming. They succumb to inordinate stress or workaholism. The victim of stress is carrying the wrong burdens. He or she is laden down with cares of the world, things they cannot change, things that should belong to someone else, things that have been or are not yet, things of lesser importance or simply too many things. The victim of workaholism may be carrying the right burdens but in the wrong way. They are driven, obsessed and out of control. They have tunnel-vision. Balance is forgotten. They are overworked in overdrive and they overheat. They put all the same essential organs at risk. They are prone to burn-out, exhaustive depression or even sudden collapse. There is no justification for such imbalance and folly. There are many warning signs and symptoms to suggest it is time for a break, a vacation, a change or simply an extended rest.

Take a moment to monitor your own life pressure. Assess the quality and strength of your passion. Is it adequate to constrain all your essential life components? Do you have strong feelings about what you really want to have, to do and to be? Can you feel the surge of interest and motivation to pursue your life's agenda? Only you can live your life. Only your passion can sustain you with joy.

How about your work habits and stress level? Have you learned the secret of inner calm? Do you carry your challenges in suitcases only when you must, setting them down when it is appropriate, or do you strap them on your back in rugsacks (back packs) and carry them all the time and everywhere? Do you have any symptoms of workaholism or imminent burn-out? Are you making time for what is truly important to you?

Respiration

The fourth and final vital sign is the quality of passive respiration or breathing. It is basic grade school hygiene to observe that *we inhale* oxygen in the air which combines with blood circulating through the lungs and from there it goes via the heart to the body's central nerve center, the brain. Within four to five minutes of losing this essential input, brain cells would begin to die irreversibly. Hypoxia or low oxygen supply is a most severe life-threatening state. It prompts immediate response with oxygen masks and pumps in order to save life. When *we exhale*, we lose more carbon dioxide and water vapor.

By analogy, your life breathes. You take in and put out on a consistent basis and the net effect is life limiting.

Into your *body* you take in nutrients and fluids to

favor optimum health and reflect a healthy image. To guide you in this area, here are my suggestions:

10 Commandments for Good Nutrition:

1. *Eat small, regular and varied meals.*
2. *Drink 6-8 glasses of fluids per day (water, juice and milk).*
3. *Reduce salt and sugar in your diet.*
4. *Run from fat.*
5. *Up your fiber.*
6. *Shop for health.*
7. *Fast (briefly) once per week.*
8. *Avoid crash diets.*
9. *Treat yourself.*
10. *Supplement your regular diet.*

Add a program of moderate exercise and optimum wellness is within your reach.   That's the product of consistent life style habit.

Into your *mind*, you feed positive thoughts.   You avoid the ubiquitous negative information, comments and opinion. You affirm what is good, what is right and what is most beneficial to you. You see the beauty, the pattern and the potential in everything.   You choose to focus on the positive realities and possibilities so you will develop a winsome attitude.   That's how you will 'have friends and influence people' most easily. Others will want to be around you, to share life, to bond and engage. You will be strengthened and empowered by this network of like-minded colleagues and acquaintances. You will never lack for attention, recognition or cooperation. This all occurs because you follow the admonition that *"whatsoever things are true, whatsoever things are honest, whatsoever things are just, whatsoever things are pure, whatsoever things are lovely, whatsoever things are of good report--if there be any virtue, and if there be any praise, think on these things"*. (St. Paul).

Finally, into your *spirit,* you welcome feelings of love to tap into a universal reservoir of infinite creative energy. Love is the most powerful force in all the world. It surpasses even faith and hope. You believe, and that's good. You anticipate the best and look forward to the future with expectation, and that too is good. But best of all, you love and cherish yourself *and* all those with whom you make contact. You welcome everyone into your space in love and that triggers sensitivity, imagination and power. Nothing can stop you now.

That is a normal and healthy life-breathing-pattern. Monitor your own *input and output* to ensure that you derive the best that life can offer.

Well, there you have it. When your best is not good enough, you first re-examine your vital signs. You make sure that you are regularly and consistently engaging in the activities that are critical for your growth and success. You seek to master your emotions and allow only the warm feelings like courage, compassion and commitment to dominate your mood and influence your behavior. You rekindle your passion, without inordinate stress, so that you are active and productive but not burning out. And then you monitor your input and output of body, mind and spirit, to favor optimum wellness, a winsome attitude and renewed creative energy. That's the first step.

Secondly, when your best is not good enough, you not only re-examine your vital signs, but you then *re-assess your assets.*

RE-ASSESS YOUR ASSETS

During the Gulf War, the world was given a crash course on military strategy and operations. Day after day and night after night, millions of television viewers sat in their own homes and listened to the Generals, the strategists and the commentators discuss the day's events on the battlefield, or more precisely, in the 'arena of conflict'. We witnessed the live action on the front lines. We watched the projectiles of guided missiles lighting up the night sky over Baghdad. We saw the arrival and devastation of 'scud' missiles near Tel Aviv. Then we observed 'patriot' anti-missiles being deployed to neutralize the threat. We saw the tanks, the maps, the fighter planes, but most of all, we saw the men and women sacrificing themselves in the arena of war for a cause their leaders sought to justify. We saw the cost of the war, the cost in human life and human suffering, the cost to civilians and their communities, the cost in military, industrial and technological terms. We saw the insanity of it all.

The 'mother of all battles' had become necessary only because the 'father of all egos' had become obsessed with ambition, disrespectful of the world community, and had badly miscalculated its resolve. Fortunately, he was forced to capitulate after his 'assets' were destroyed. With near surgical precision, the allies took out military command headquarters, bomb factories, germ warfare establishments, and a nation's infrastructure. Huge casualties in the arena threatened the survival of the regime in Baghdad.

The language and strategy of the military brass should teach us all a lesson. Before the assault on Baghdad was initiated, the allied nations assembled a most formidable force of half a million fighters, complemented with the most sophisticated military hardware ever deployed. These 'assets' were overwhelming and more than adequate to get the job done. Then, and only then, could the success of 'Desert Storm' be guaranteed. Officers and reporters gave daily accounts of the cost in 'assets' continually. They valued them and depended on them to win the war.

Now for the lesson. At the height of the Gulf War, Israel became a target for Iraqi 'scud' missiles. The entire population was threatened and therefore fearful and paranoid about the imminent threat. Despite the magnitude of the sophisticated 'assets' on the ground in the region at that time, there was a strategic window of weakness remaining. The allies had done their best to this point, but it was not good enough. It became necessary to reassess all their assets. Within days, United States 'patriot' missiles were being airlifted to the arena to counter the underestimated threat from the mobile 'scud' missile launchers that could, in principle, be delivered almost anywhere and at any time in that region. The solution was to reassess *all available assets* and to deploy whatever was necessary to immobilize the enemy. There were adequate 'assets' available to get the job done and they did it.

The lesson is both personal and practical. When you feel you have done your best and your best is not good enough, it is time, urgent time, to reassess all your available assets.   Chances are that you will have in reserve latent resources not yet deployed to your advantage. Choose any category you wish and begin there.

Think of your brain. Just when you begin to believe that you have run out of ideas or peaked in your analysis or insight into a problem or situation, it is time to think again. The best of us will use a small fraction of our brain. The rest will return to the earth unused, untapped, unknown. Therefore, there is always room for new ideas, for reconsideration, for brainstorming, and imagination. After a conscious re-creative break from the problem, it makes sense to take a fresh look, a new approach, an alternative model. Think, then think again. Think laterally, think tangentially, think creatively, but think. Gather new information, rearrange input data, seek out new references, ask for expert opinion, thrash things out, 'doodle' if necessary, but persevere until a solution is found.

Think of your time. Like most of us, you probably never have enough of that commodity. 'So much to do, and so little time'. So you do your best, you work as hard and as efficiently as you can, but you just can't seem to get everything done. You seem to lose the battle daily, weekly, monthly, annually, and you sometimes fear you might lose it altogether with a long final list of all that 'could have been done' if you only had more time. Now it's time to reassess your use of time.

It has been pointed out that 'time management' is a misnomer, for time cannot be managed. It is an autonomous flux of change that flows from one moment to the next, irrespective of everything else. We can only manage *our lives* in that changing dimension. So 'time management' is more accurately defined as 'life management'. Recall the work of Stephen Covey and the paradigm of *importance* superseding *urgency*. To reassess your time, is to reassess your values, your focus, your commitments. It is to explore how to improve your personal efficiency and more so, how to tap into the time and therefore the life of other colleagues and acquaintances. It is increased delegation of duties, improved cooperation and partnership, and internalized priorities. Reassess your time.

Think of your financial assets. Who would not like to be more financially secure? To have the means at one's disposal to do whatever one chooses, at least the activities that money can buy. Those for whom money is no object, who have true financial independence, have other problems. They may struggle with motivation, with fulfillment, with boredom, with paranoia, with guilt, with a hundred and one other challenges. But they are not the focus here. We are more concerned about the person who is trying their best to get ahead economically. They are struggling to finance a principal residence for the family, or a small business proposition, or a college education. If you work hard, you save, you spend judiciously and you still have monetary anxiety, if not hardship, then it's time to reassess your real assets.

It's time to reconsider your sources of income and how that can be changed. New income possibilities must be high on your agenda. It's time to look again at your leveraging portfolio. Can you put any reserve or fluid asset to work? Is there access to capital that you can multiply through investment or leverage? Is there anything you could liquidate or convert to higher net return? Lack of money is very seldom the true bottleneck to success. There is usually a source , a means, a way forward if you are seeking one.

What is it that you dream of? What is the struggle in which you are engaged? You are doing your apparent best and your best is not enough. So what next? Reassess *all* your assets. Put your brain, your time, your money, your contacts, your leverage, your personality, your reputation ... put them all to work for you. What about referrals and networking? Think of information sources and counselors. Dig deep for your inner strengths and latent skills. Take advantage of your unique qualities, your particular blend, your singular combination of skills and experience. Bring all your assets to the front lines and fight to win. Engage your real worth in pursuit of real success. You will get better, you will grow stronger and eventually, you will triumph victoriously.

Finally, when your best is not good enough, you should not only re-examine your vital signs, and re-assess your assets, but you should also *re-adjust your focus.*

RE-ADJUST YOUR FOCUS

Contemporary life is so demanding, and at times, even overwhelming. Given the increased awareness of what's happening in the world and what is available, and given the challenges of modern communications and transportation technology, we make very high demands on ourselves. The typical person putting in a normal day's work, will feel unaccomplished and uninspired because of the haunting realization of all else that is possible, if one puts their mind to initiate and produce more. You have access to so much information and opportunity that you can ill afford to be self-satisfied or at ease with mediocre achievement of any kind.

Therefore you are prone to engage a wide variety of streams into your life. You have information and ideas, challenges and responsibilities, as well as demands and expectations, bombarding you from all sides. It is as if you are being pushed and pulled in every direction, whether it be at work, at home or in the market place. No sooner do you seem to be settling down and getting in to some groove or other, then you hear a clarion call beckoning you to change. Or you feel the shifting sands beneath your feet signaling the imminent change. Or at worst, you are catapulted by the forces of change. The only constant in life today is change itself. So some would argue that you must be prepared. 'Don't put your eggs in one basket' we are told. 'Keep all options open. Be slow to burn any of your bridges. Live cautiously. Be prepared for the worst. Don't specialize too soon, if at all.'

Businesses have tried to adapt to changing market forces. They have attempted to broaden their appeal to increase market share. They have sought to diversify to maintain client loyalty. But it has not worked. Whether you consider huge automobile manufacturers, computer giants or hamburger chains, the results show that companies that remained focused and true to their traditional image, their unique persona, have emerged better and stronger for it.

Contrast, for example, the case of Pepsi Co and Coca-Cola. Pepsi Co has twice the sales and assets of Coca-Cola-- yet Coke's stock is worth more than twice that of Pepsi's. Why? Coca-Cola focuses on its core business--that of selling soft drinks. Pepsi Co has drifted from its focus and is now selling soft drinks, tea and snack foods, while also importing vodka and running separate fast-food restaurant chains that sell pizza, tacos and chicken.

That's an amazing contrast.

IBM is another classic. The company made a ton of money when it focused on mainframe computers. Then it drifted into selling mid-range computers, workstations, desktop and home computers, software and the like. Its profits crashed as it launched one sputtering business after another, from copiers to Rolm to Satellite Business Systems to Prodigy to SAA to TopView to Office Vision to OS/2 Warp. Changes in technology allowed specialists to focus on narrow parts of the computer market that once belonged to IBM. These smaller companies were superior in their niche and cut deep into market share.

One further illustration. In the automobile industry, companies that have maintained a consistent focus and image, have fought off competition successfully. Volvo, from its inception, focused on *safety* and continues to do so. It is the largest selling imported luxury car in America, ahead of BMW and Mercedes-Benz for a decade. Or consider the diversity of General Motors. The two divisions with the tightest focus are Saturn and Cadillac, on two opposite ends of the market. Saturn is built on one platform, is available in one model with one engine and one transmission. The average Saturn dealer sold 960 cars in the U.S. in 1994. That is 47 percent more than the runner-up, Honda, with 651 cars per dealer. Contrast the 36 percent decline in annual sales of Chevy models between 1984 and 1994. The average Chevy dealer has such a broad line of vehicles, designed to appeal to every buyer, but sells only 226 per year. What is a Chevy today? Blurr ...

The point is that when a company loses focus, its identity becomes blurred in the minds of consumers, and managers too are distracted from paying attention to the core business. Often decision-makers forget, or ignore the fact, that a business is often successful because it was focused on a single, highly profitable product, service or market. They want to appeal to everybody, they want to diversify and expand. But they branch out and become spread too thin. The energy and sense of direction disappear, and before long, the company's objectives are missed, sales flatten, profits decline and panic strikes.

To re-adjust your focus is to maximize your efficiency in three distinct areas. Each can be clearly illustrated by a common example from everyday life.

The first reason to re-adjust is to get a *true picture*.

You focus for *clarity*. The art of photography and imaging technology, including video images, is to arrange lighting, lenses and length of exposure so that one can reproduce clear images as close to the original as possible. Even the amateur photographer understands that to get a clear picture, it is most important to focus the camera. You adjust the variables until you can see the reality you seek to reproduce with maximum clarity. Failure to adjust the aperture or the lens or the time of exposure is to make a poor, distorted and blurred copy of the original. The image on a television screen implies the same thing. You can fine-tune the adjustments until the picture is sharp and in focus. Then you see it most clearly. Then you can discern the fine detail. Then you can enjoy the picture for all it is worth.

When you are doing your best and your best is not enough, it is time to re-adjust for clarity. You must seek to improve your vision and perception. Try to gain better perspective and insight. Aim to see the complete picture, in balance, without distortion and exaggeration. You are prone, over time, to get life out of focus. Your margins become blurred, your colors confused and your scale irregular. You soon find that you major in minor things and neglect things of real importance. You make loose associations and assign incorrect labels. So you see challenges as problems, opportunities as risks, negativism as realism, and selfishness as success. That's what happens when you focus on problems, on risks, on negativity and worst of all, on yourself. Then it is time to readjust for clarity until you can truly perceive the challenge of opportunity and the realism of true success.

Many companies today are spending a lot of time and manpower to clearly identify both Mission and Vision statements. The intent is to articulate these for all managers, employees and clients, so that everyone can know exactly what the company is about. It defines a focus of clarity. You too can do well to define your own personal mission and vision. That will bring your life into focus and help to keep it there.

The second reason to re-adjust your focus, is to maximize *accuracy*. **You focus for precision**. The common picture is that of the superb marksman who takes very careful aim of the bull's eye. He brings it into clear focus and then releases for his target. Precision bombing describes the careful, guided delivery of the 'asset' to strike exactly the desired target. It is not indiscriminate or haphazard.

For the neurosurgeon, operating under the magnification of an optical eye piece, precision surgery demands the careful identification of minute anatomical structures, with good understanding and appreciation of the identity and function of each one. Then he or she must execute surgical procedure with painstaking accuracy to eventually maximize function for the patient. To miss could sometimes mean paralysis or even death.

For generations the Swiss dominated the art of watchmaking. They had mastered the principles of physics inherent in springs, coils and cog wheels to make beautiful precision watches as reliable as one could want. They became obsessed with their technology and when the invention of oscillating quartz was introduced, they turned their backs, only to find later that the superior quartz technology would well near put them out of business. They failed to make the necessary 'paradigm shift'. It is never enough to focus so intently on one thing, that you become blinded or immune to alternative possibilities and suggestions. The focus of precision implies exactness, diligence, resonance and carefulness. It does not imply tunnel vision or egocentrisms. You must never lock-in. You must reserve the right to shift precisely when it's necessary, and only precisely because it is the right thing to do.

When you are doing your best and your best is not enough, it is time to re-adjust for precision. You must take another look at your target, examine for fine detail, plan and strategize for maximum effectiveness and then deliver with care. You can never take things for granted. You must never fall asleep at the helm of your life. You cannot afford to assume or presume too much. You must remain vigilant and deliberate in all you seek to do. The lives of others may depend on it.

A third reason to re-adjust your focus is to concentrate *power*. **You focus for intensity**. The energy of the sun radiates continuously and it pierces the clouds to bathe the earth with a shower of light and heat. This is life sustaining. But most of the time it is a quiet phenomenon. On a given day, visible light, with ultraviolet and infrared radiation in the tails of its spectrum, strikes the earth without any drama or sensation. Of course, the annual spontaneous bush fires in many parts of the world are a constant reminder of the power of solar energy. And the prevalence of skin cancer in unfortunate and careless sun worshippers also underlines that there is more to this exposure than meets the eye. However, it is still uncommon on any given day, to see the direct effect of the sun's rays.

That is so until a small schoolboy gets his way. He finds a small magnifying glass and grabs a piece of paper, before running outside to his primitive but powerful natural physics laboratory. All he needs to do for this common demonstration is to hold his magnifying glass above the piece of paper as he makes the adjustment. He holds the glass to lie across the direction of the sun's rays, he holds the paper flat or parallel to the glass, then he slowly adjusts the distance between them. First he sees a circle of light. As he moves the paper or glass away, the diameter of the circle gets smaller until it converges to a small point and then something most dramatic happens. Yes, a fire! The paper burns. The diffuse latent energy of the sun's rays, when focused on a specific point, causes a fire to ignite. That is the power of focus. Whenever we focus, we create intensity and intensity creates fire. And fire...

When you are doing your best and your best is not enough, it is time to re-adjust for intensity. To consciously decide on a given objective, to define a precise goal, to bring the streams of life to flow into a single channel, is to create intensity. To give priority to a specific task at hand, to choose an activity that you value enough to neglect lesser duties, to commit to a singular enterprise, is also to create intensity. To shut out distraction, eliminate vacillation and embrace your project with determination, is again to create intensity. Intensity creates fire; fire in the bosom to energize and motivate the focused individual; fire in the personality to empower and attract all that is needed for cooperation and production; and then fire in the surroundings as the conflagration spreads to add light and heat to others and make a big difference in the world.

Focus for clarity, focus for precision and focus for intensity. Continually readjust your focus.

So when you have done your best and your best is still not good enough, you must remember that for things to change, you must change; for things to get better, you must get better. You can be better than your existing best.

To that end, you need to re-examine your vital signs: your consistency of action (your pulse), your warm feelings (your temperature), the intensity of your passion and the level and style of your productivity (your systolic and diastolic pressures), and finally, your input and output of body, mind and spirit (your respiration).

Then you need to re-assess all your assets and harness them to maximum advantage. Tap more of your brain. Manage your life and therefore your time. Leverage all your economic assets for what they are worth. Utilize your contacts and every other resource at your disposal.

Most importantly, re-adjust your focus for clarity, precision and intensity to cause the fire to burn and the conflagration to spread, to bring the difference of light and heat to your immediate surroundings.

Then you can truly exclaim **YES!** and prove that it is really worth it. You will have arrived ... but not quite, unless you are given to complete *abandon.* Go on to the climax.

*   *   *

The Evolution of **YES!** *unfolds:*

You must risk participation
as you pursue your dream,
without excuse now,
by making a clear decision
to be bold enough and commit to
becoming!

12

ABANDON

("YES!!! I'll do it even if it kills me")

Congratulations!

You have now completed *The Evolution of* **YES!** and indeed, your life has become an exclamation of **YES!**

Let's briefly review the twelve Phases that you have mastered along the journey. They are more cumulative than sequential since none is truly left behind. You will continue to grow in each of these dimensions all the time, for you can always get better. But you can take pride even now in what you have already achieved.

You have discovered who you are and what you are all about in this world. You know you can have, you can do and you can be whatever you choose, now that you have set your mind to it. You refuse to stand on the sidelines anymore, for you are now constrained from within by a true sense of vocation. You can do no less.

There are no conditional qualifications in your

response to life either, for you will take the calculated risk. You will consider all the alternatives available, weigh your real options and then go for it. While others only wish and hope for something better, you have focused the power of your imagination to design the life you choose and all excuses have been cheerfully set aside.

Today your sense of urgency obscures tomorrow, so you cherish the present moment and you will therefore act now. That you will do, not with ambivalence or duplicity, but decisively and resolutely. You now know that it is your inalienable right to pursue your dream and to experience success. And *that* you have defined in your own terms. So you are prepared to ask, to seek and to knock on every door of opportunity at your disposal.

You say **YES!** without the hesitation and trepidation of the proverbial schoolboy's try. You are committed, with no reservations whatever, and even when your best efforts prove inadequate, you will continue to grow and to get better. In a word, you will pursue your goals with a reckless abandon as if everything depended on them. You will spare no quarter in the passionate pursuit of excellence.

To that end you will consistently -

Think **YES!**

Say **YES!**

and *Live* **YES!**

THINK YES!

Your secret weapon is in your mind for there you have taken control. You refuse to succumb to the pattern of negative influences in the environment. You neglect or reject all such negative ideas and information, from whatever source and no matter how popular they may be. Instead, you choose to focus on the positive aspects of every situation and to maintain an optimistic expectation for the future.

Like Norman Vincent Peale has written, *The Power of Positive Thinking* has been released within you as an explosive force for change and achievement. As you consciously elect to think **YES!** you find a new perspective on your circumstances. You have come to believe--to believe in yourself, your future, your world, and perhaps your Maker. All skepticism and cynicism have followed negativism through the door and now you have the sweet comfort of assurance.

There is a buoyancy and an energy that gives you confidence and resilience as you face the challenges ahead. When you think **YES!** you can remain calm in the midst of turbulence and uncertainty. You feel stronger than ever and you will move forward with conviction and purposefulness. You are empowered to influence others and to make a real difference in your world.

But your thoughts go beyond just attitude and assurance. They generate activity. Like Robert Schueller has written, you can now *Move Ahead With* **Possibility Thinking**. Between your ears, resides the greatest generator of power in the world. From that seat of consciousness, reason and imagination you can order your new reality into being. It is a power akin to the Divine, to create something out of nothing. It begins with seeing or conceiving that possibility in the mind.

So you now cultivate dreams that surpass all previous experience. You crystallize goals that electrify you and draw unexpected streams of blessing into your life. And you carve solutions to problems and difficulties because you are focused sharply on the myriad of possibilities at any given moment.

Your thinking has obviously matured after reading through this book. So you are now invited to go beyond *positive* thinking, and even beyond *possibility* thinking, to discover on an elevated plane, that there is something more:

The Pride of **Positional Thinking**.

To think YES! is
　　　　to adopt a certain position,
　　　　to defend some core principles and
　　　　to find for yourself a clear purpose.

Positional Thinking *is therefore to take a stand for a pattern of life and behavior that makes you remain* *unmoveable, always abounding in* **the** *work that you now love to do. You have locked in on what is important and your mind-set anchors you to that ground.*

Your conviction is passionate. Your position is clear and firm. Your commitment is unconditional. You know exactly where you stand. You therefore stand tall.

Whatever your circumstance may be just now, and no matter what the challenge you fear or the opportunity you face, you have carved out a position in your mind that gives you the elusive anchor of both security and serenity. That is the affirmative posture you take. It is the personal resolution that you make. You are constrained by your principles and your sense of purpose. It is your right to live. It is your life to choose ... **YES!**

From that base you can then leverage all your imaginative powers to see beyond your immediate horizon. You can generate solutions. You can create change. You can continue to grow. That is **Positional Thinking.**

From that vantage point you can now *say* **YES!**

SAY YES!

You understand the power of words. In them lies the power of life and death.

Words of encouragement and hope enable the weak and faint to carry on when everything else says 'give up and die'.

Words of heroism make young men and women run bravely into bullets.

Spoken in season, kind words build bridges across the chasms of human misunderstanding to touch the heart. But out of season, harsh words tear the most intimate relationships apart.

Gentle words can bring comfort in times of deepest pain and despair, while insensitive words cause wounds, too deep for any echoes to appear.

It is not the quantity of words that constitute their magic and power, it is their quality. It is the form and content that conveys their meaning and empowers them like guided missiles to release incredible power when they strike their intended target. Therefore they are to be launched with care.

Words are often self-fulfilling prophecies. The things you say empower you or else disarm you in the struggle of life. You are never the same on the other side of conscious confession. Each utterance is a contribution to the unfolding reality of your own world and runs a fiber as it were, in the tapestry of your own life. And it is irreversible. Of the 'three things that come not back', the unknown author noted first *'the spoken word,'* then was added 'the sped arrow and the neglected opportunity.'

In *Genesis*, the book of beginnings, all of creation is described in language that suggests there is fundamental value and power in self-expression. There it is written, time and time again, "And God said... and it was so". It is as if in the very *word* of God, resides the very *power* of God.

If that were not enough, in the gospel of *John*, the book of new beginnings, the language is reminiscent and the Greek word '*Logos*' is used to refer to the transcendent Son. He is the eternal living *Word*, the divine effulgence, not unlike the spoken word. But He is distinguished when He "became flesh, and dwelt among us".

And grasp this, "the *Word* of the Lord abides forever"--the living Word and the spoken word.

It is not surprising that of all creation, the attribute of verbal communication is given only to *homo sapiens*. Humans alone reflect the essence of that divine image in qualities of self-consciousness, reason and verbal communication. We alone are charged to take dominion and to actively participate in the on-going unfolding of creation.

What a privilege!

By our words we can, in part, effect our part. We can both create change and order the direction of that change. We are invited not only to speak to the Throne of grace above, but also to address the *mountains* that stand in our path below, as well as to confess the *faults* that dog our steps, and so to progress beyond them both.

Oh, what power in our words!

The life of **YES!** implies more than thinking. It

involves speaking. Words constitute both the process and the product of such a positive, passionate and productive experience.

May I invite you to do something more. Go back through *The Evolution of YES!* and extract all the useful affirmations that you can use for active confession. Say them aloud and repeat them as often as you need, to generate the internal dynamic of such self-fulfilling expressions. Begin with those words if you choose, and add to them, but use your choice words as a source of inspiration and an agent for change in your own life.

As you consistently reiterate words of affirmation, these simple creations of the brain will traverse the all important eighteen inches to the heart. There they will connect with passion, desire and commitment to become explosive forces of human energy that can transform your world. They become more than words or even ideas. They will become fountains of inner strength and resilience that will allow you to face all the challenges of life. They will allow you to see and to seize opportunity as never before. You will therefore grow by leaps and bounds.

That is the transforming magic of affirmation. Try it!

As you continue to grow, be careful of your own words. Accentuate the positive and eliminate the negative. Affirm others just as you affirm yourself.

Keep saying **YES!**

In the face of challenge, you must affirm 'Yes, I can'. In the face of opportunity, again you must affirm 'Yes, I will'. Let there be no 'if's', no 'and's', no 'but's' ... just an unadulterated '**YES!**' It is your life to *confess* ... **YES!**

In every response, look for and choose the preamble, the position or the prospect that leads you to say **YES!** You will find a big difference. You will make an even bigger difference.

When you think about it, that's the only exciting way to live ... to *live* **YES!**

LIVE YES!

Way back there in Phase One, we observed that there is a renewed emphasis today on the term 'quality of life' and all that it implies. The concern is not just as it relates to the senior citizens, as we follow the age wave sweeping in time across the culture. Nor is it just for the terminally ill, now that modern medicine has managed to sustain and prolong the last phase of life to sometimes ridiculous extremes.

But even for the active baby-boomers and those who follow in their wake, this is a time of much social upheaval. Major changes are occurring in the home and in the workplace. Families are being challenged on every front. Everyone seems busier than ever. New technologies are changing our daily routines and responsibilities so that nothing can be taken for granted, including even where, when and how we choose to live and work. No wonder then that many fundamental questions about quality of life have resurfaced.

Some analysts have tried to measure the consequences of this modern change in terms of variables such as leisure, security, income shifts, and the like. These all tend to be 'bread and butter' issues. But life is more than 'bread and butter'. To live **YES!** is to go far beyond the basic necessities of life.

For anyone who must still be concerned with subsistence on a daily basis, they would do well to go back and study *The Evolution of* **YES!** again. They should find their foothold to spring up and climb out of such circumstance. There is too much bounty and opportunity in the world (at least in *your* world, if you have the privilege of reading this book) to continue a life of just making ends meet.

In the face of free enterprise and with the time, hopefully the health, and the skill-set that you must have, the ideas contained in this book are enough to spur you into action and to cause even the 'down and out' to move up and be included among the 'up and in' crowd. You too can come to say **YES!** and to live **YES!**

Now, for those readers who dare to consider the life of **YES!**, you will perceive that it is a progressive growth experience in the *Hierarchy of Why*. You first go beyond subsistence, then you move from the social constraints of pride, social acceptance and dignity, to the more personal values of freedom, fulfillment and self-actualization.

Ultimately, the life of **YES!** affirms a strong sense of purpose. You should come to find your place in the world, like the reason and meaning for your existence, and you could take delight in expressing it to the fullest. You would therefore live a life that is resolute and confident.

To live **YES!** is to choose on a daily basis to squeeze from every moment of time, the last drop of possibility. It is to harness all personal resources to advantage and to develop a keen sense of vocation and destiny. That must include giving as much as receiving. You will go beyond mere self interest to seek to make a difference in your world. You will therefore find a spontaneous desire to make each day significant and to pursue excellence without compromise. You want to win but not at all cost. You value playing at the game of life even more than you enjoy attaining the prize. So you engage with reckless abandon.

There is no stopping you now.

You are assured of your own space and so you can make room for all others. This makes for mutual respect and healthy relationships around you. You are now no longer surprised by the generosity of others.

You get back what you give out.

But you are never coy and self-satisfied. You feel like you have only just begun. You welcome each day with eager anticipation for what you are becoming and the opportunity and challenge it affords you to grow, to give and to serve.

To live **YES!** is therefore to live on tip-toe, with your eyes peering over the horizon and your arms outstretched to embrace this moment. Your mind will be at peace but you will be imagining what could yet be, as your heart remains wide open to the world.

This is a life of passion and excitement, a life of vision with integrity. There is no simpler way to put it... it is the life of **YES!** It is your life to *confirm* ... **YES!**

Just live it.

Think **YES!!**

Say   **YES!!**

Live   **YES!!**

Dr. YES!

The Evolution of **YES!** *unfolds:*

You must risk participation
as you pursue your dream,
without excuse now,
by making a clear decision
to be bold enough
and commit to becoming
one who lives with abandon
the exclamation of

YES!!!

● — ● — ● — ● — ● — ● — ● — ● — ● — ● — ●

In the *now...*

and in the *end* ...

YES!!!

ORDER FORM

Please rush me the following books:

		Quantity		Each	
☐	GE-10	_____	The "YES!" Trilogy (3 books) @	$54.95	_____
☐	GE-12	_____	Your Evolution to YES!	$23.95	_____
☐	GE-13	_____	Understanding the Evolution of YES!	$19.95	_____
☐	GE-14	_____	Evolutionary Tales from **Dr. YES!**	$16.95	_____
☐	GE-5	_____	A Passion For Living	$ 4.99	_____

Total Amount of Order $_____

Telephone orders: Call Toll Free: 1(800) 501-8516

Postal Orders: ProMotion Publishing,
2778 Hargrove Road, Suite: 206
Smyrna, GA 30080

Fax Orders: 1-770-801-0304

☐   Please send the above books to:

Company name:_____

Name:_____

Address:_____ Suite No._____

City_____ State_____

Zip: _____-_____ Telephone: (_____)_____

Sales tax:
Georgia residents add sales tax.

Shipping/Handling
"The **YES!** *Trilogy"* $6.95 each set. All other books add $2.50 per book.

Payment:
☐   Visa   ☐ Mastercard   Name on card:_____
☐   Card #:_____ Expiry Date_____
☐   Money order/Certified Check Enclosed
☐   Check

Call toll free **and order NOW.**

NOTES

ORDER FORM - Canadian Residents

Please rush me the following books:

		Quantity		Each	
☐	GE-10	_____	The "YES!" Trilogy (3 books) @	$58.95	_____
☐	GE-12	_____	Your Evolution to YES!	$26.95	_____
☐	GE-13	_____	Understanding the Evolution of YES!	$21.95	_____
☐	GE-14	_____	Evolutionary Tales from Dr. YES!	$18.95	_____
☐	GE-5	_____	A Passion For Living	$ 6.99	_____

Total Amount of Order $_____

Telephone orders: Call Toll Free: 1(800) 501-8516

Postal Orders: ProMotion Publishing,
                2778 Hargrove Road, Suite 206,
                Smyrna, GA 30080
Fax Orders: 1-770-801-0304

☐   Please send the above books to:

Company name:_____

Name:_____

Address:_____ Suite No._____

City_____ State_____

Postal Code: _____ Telephone: (_____)_____

Add Sales tax (GST/PST):

Shipping:
*"The **YES!** Trilogy"* $6.95 each set. All other books add $2.50 per book.

☐   Visa   ☐ Mastercard   Name on card:_____
      Card #:_____ Expiry Date_____
☐   Money order/Certified Check Enclosed
☐   Check

Call toll free and order NOW.

NOTES

NOTES